The

OCCASIONAL
VEGAN

For Mum

The
OCCASIONAL VEGAN

Sarah Philpott

SEREN

is the book imprint of
Poetry Wales Press Ltd.
57 Nolton Street, Bridgend, Wales, CF31 3AE

www.serenbooks.com
facebook.com/SerenBooks
twitter: @SerenBooks

© Sarah Philpott, 2018
Photographs © Manon Houston, 2018

The right of Sarah Philpott to be identified
as the author of this work has been asserted
in accordance with the Copyright,
Designs and Patents Act, 1988.

ISBN 978-1-78172-431-6

A CIP record for this title is available
from the British Library.

The publisher works with the financial
assistance of the Welsh Books Council.

Cover photograph: © Manon Houston,
www.manonhouston.com

Printed in the Czech Republic
by Akcent Media Ltd.

Contents

Introduction

The recipes

Introduction

'There is no love sincerer than the love of food' – *George Bernard Shaw*

My voyage into veganism

This is a vegan cookbook, but really it's the story of my love of cooking and eating. Unlike many cooks and writers, I'm not posh. I'm from a pretty humble background and when I was growing up, my mum was a single parent with a full-time job who put dinner on the table every night. Mum started my love affair with food and in this book, I recreate some of my favourite childhood meals from when I was growing up in Wales during the 1990s.

I've always loved food and feel sorry for people who don't seem to like it. Eating should be a joy. Perhaps that's a privileged thing to say, but for me flavours and feelings go hand in hand and food is tied up in so many of our formative experiences. Food is there during our most memorable rites of passage. For me, the smell of burgers brings back memories of student barbeques, drunk on cheap rosé. Tucking into a Chinese takeaway takes me back to Saturday night sleepovers as a teenager. For many of us, a meal is a memory – and sometimes a friend, too.

I think about food a lot and like most people, my days are punctuated by mealtimes. From childhood, to adolescence, through school and university, boyfriends and break ups, mealtimes have always been a constant for me.

I grew up without a dad so my mum had to be mother and father to my sisters and me. It wasn't quite kitchen sink drama but it wasn't all sugar and spice either. Life wasn't perfect but a lot of Mum's love and nurture was expressed through her cooking.

I can picture it now: bubbling saucepans, music blaring, Mum's terrible dancing. Money was tight but we ate adventurously and with gusto. Mum always made sure that there was a decent dinner on the table and bought the best ingredients she could afford.

Holding down a full-time job meant that Mum didn't always have time to cook, though. Some of my favourite food memories include snuggling up with spoonfuls of Heinz tomato soup and buttered white bread and stirring Sacla pesto into deep bowls of spaghetti. While other kids tucked into Birds Eye potato waffles, Mum's interest in food meant that we tucked into vast amounts of houmous and pesto when they hit the supermarkets in the 1990s.

As a chubby kid at the cusp of adolescence, I used food as a comfort blanket. I wasn't very cool at school: although academically adequate, I was terrible at sport and I was shy and gawky. I wasn't unpopular but food was my best friend. I ate through the events of the late nineties: Tony Blair's triumphant Labour Party, Princess Diana's death, Girl Power, fear of the Millennium Bug.

When I wasn't at school, I spent my time with my head in a book or glued to the screen as celebrity cooks like Nigella Lawson and Jamie Oliver burst onto the scene. The foodies I saw on TV and in books were mostly posh, unlike me, but they definitely spoke my language as they whipped up a casserole or crème brûlée; it was proper comfort viewing.

So how did I get here? How does such a big eater end up eating what many think of as rabbit food? It started, as many things do, at the end of a chapter in my life. At the tail end of my twenties, I reached a crossroads. I was facing the big 3-0, had broken up with a long-term boyfriend and was wondering what the hell to do with my life. Although I enjoyed my job at a charity, I knew it wasn't 'the one'. I was a bit lost, I guess.

In the year that I turned thirty, the feeling that something wasn't quite right kept niggling at me; I needed a change. Veganism was in the news and I realised that I'd been turning a blind eye to the plight of animals, not just the ones killed for their meat but also the horrific conditions of the dairy and poultry industry. I was a fully-fledged omnivore but I knew it was time to act. Never one to do things by halves, I decided to go cold turkey and become vegan.

My friends and family scoffed at the idea. You'll never keep it up, they told me. I was the girl who ate the fat off bacon, the chicken skin, had extra butter on her toast. Yes, I ate everything.

I've always had what Mum called a 'healthy appetite'. I will eat under all circumstances, whether I'm glad, mad or sad. I've done my fair share of comfort eating: bread and white carbs after arguments with my mum and a liquid diet of soup, wine and gin in times of heartbreak.

There have been times when food has been more foe than friend. If I felt bored or lonely, I'd head straight for the biscuit barrel. That initial burst of dopamine soon descended into dread. Sometimes it got to the point where I was sick of eating but a slave to food. I was constantly thinking about what I should and shouldn't eat, counting calories, and starting and stopping diets. Eating a plant-based diet has brought a certain peace to my body and mind because it makes sense to me.

This is the story of my voyage into veganism. I love my food more than ever these days. I'm a home cook, not a professional chef, but I'm passionate about inspiring others to eat well, simply, cheaply and above all, creatively, and that's why I've written this book. My recipes are all easy to make and many are inspired by the food my mother cooked for me as a child; this is proper home cooking and I promise you that you'll want seconds.

What is this book?

As we all know, the last couple of years have seen a huge rise in the number of people who choose a vegan lifestyle, whether that's full-time or just mindfully cutting back on animal produce. If you're either of these people or if you simply love food, this book is for you.

Veganism is having a moment, perhaps because we are a lot more conscious about animal welfare and about mitigating climate change. At the last count, there were over half a million vegans in the UK – that's an increase of 350% in the last ten years – and people are enjoying the benefits: it's kinder to animals and the environment, and it's also gentler on your body – and your wallet.

This book takes a holistic approach to eating well. Eating a diet of plants and grains is good for your physical and mental wellbeing and also helps to look after the wider world. Going vegan means ditching meat and fish, as vegetarians do, and also eggs, dairy and honey – but that doesn't mean giving up on flavoursome food.

If you're vegan, you're probably reading this because you're keen to try some new recipes. If you're curious about this way of eating, then welcome! Keep reading because I'm not here to convert you to veganism. Eating a plant-based diet is something that you can do part-time or one day a week, if you want to, and this book will help you create simple, nourishing and delicious meals using inexpensive ingredients. Prepare to be excited about eating and to get creative in the kitchen.

In this book, you'll find meals for every occasion, whether that's a quick weeknight supper, a leisurely weekend brunch, or something for a special celebration. I will show you that a plant-based diet (whether that's as a fully-fledged vegan or by simply following this lifestyle one or two days a week) can make you healthy and happy – and that you really can have your cake and eat it.

So, why should you try eating vegan?

There are some real benefits to eating this way and these are just some of them.

- It's delicious – and you won't get bored. Eating a rainbow of fruits and vegetables as well as a multitude of grains, pulses and nuts will inspire you to be a lot more creative in the kitchen. I must make it clear that these recipes do not try to replicate meaty meals; they are tasty dishes in their own right. It's a real shame that we don't value vegetables and I hope that these recipes make you think differently about them. One of my favourite meals is cauliflower roasted in a little olive oil and some cumin seeds and lemon zest with wilted greens, brown rice, a generous squeeze of lemon juice and a smattering of toasted flaked almonds. Now that's luxury for you.

- It's cheap, and easier than ever before. As well as improving your health, it will save you money. This book shows you what to buy and where to shop to get the best ingredients you can afford. If done properly, going vegan (or eating less animal produce) is easy on the wallet so let's debunk the myth that eating well comes at a cost.

- It's kinder to your body – be that your skin, digestion, weight, or energy levels. There's no way to sugar the pill: too much meat is bad for our bodies. As well as making your digestion sluggish, it's a carcinogenic. A study of 500,000 people by the National Cancer Institute found that those who ate the most red meat daily were 30% more likely to die of any cause during a ten-year period than those who ate the least amount. I'm not telling you to stop eating meat, but you might want to think about cutting down.

- It's kinder to animals. Let's not beat around the bush here: many of us turn a blind eye, not only to the cruelty of the meat industry, but also to the suffering of animals bred for eggs and dairy. Every week in the UK, 3,000 male calves are taken away days after birth, and are either shot or exported alive to mainland European countries where they are kept in small pens to produce veal flesh. You can imagine the heartache their mothers go through and they can often be heard calling for their calves for days afterwards. That's just one part of their miserable lives because after their calves have been taken away from them, mother cows are hooked up, two or more times a day, to milking machines. They're then impregnated by artificial insemination every year and so the cycle repeats itself. These cows usually only live for five years (the average lifespan is twenty years) because they're so worn out from this inflicted cruelty. When they are killed, their bodies are often in such a sorry state that they can only be used for ground meat and pet food.

- Let's not forget the 40 million day-old chicks who are killed each year, and yes, that includes those from organic farms. Male chicks are of no use for egg or meat production, and almost immediately after hatching, they are thrown into an industrial grinder while still alive or gassed to death. Their mothers don't fare much better. Regardless of whether they're in free range (where as many as nine birds can occupy one square metre of floor space) or caged farming systems, hens lead an existence of pain and suffering throughout their shortened lives. All commercial hens are sent to slaughter after around one year's egg production despite having a natural life span of seven years.

- Let's talk about the environment. Did you know that it takes 2,500 litres of water (that's the equivalent of 32 showers) to make just one hamburger? Or that cows produce 150 billion gallons of methane, which is up to 100 times more destructive than carbon dioxide, every day? Raising animals for food is the largest source of greenhouse gases, and the use and degradation of land. It's the number one source of water pollution and rainforest deforestation and it's also a major contributor to air pollution, ocean dead zones, habitat loss, and species extinction.

- Roughly one billion people on the planet are malnourished and six million children starve to death every year and yet half of the world's edible grain crop is fed to farm animals. When you consider that one acre of land can produce 250 pounds of beef compared to 50,000 pounds of tomatoes or 53,000 pounds of potatoes, it's blindingly obvious how wasteful meat and dairy farming can be.

A word about wellness…

There has been a lot of debate about the term 'wellness' over the last few years but what exactly does it mean? The Oxford English Dictionary defines it as 'the quality or state of being in good health, especially as an actively pursued goal'. So, is wellness simply the act of looking after your health? If so, it all sounds perfectly fine in theory – but it can go too far. Yes, I'm talking about clean eating.

Thankfully there's been some backlash against this diet because restricting food groups is utterly joyless and it can be dangerous, too. As Nigella Lawson says, "food is not dirty" and should be enjoyed in moderation. In the wrong hands, clean eating can encourage an obsession with food and can potentially lead to eating disorders.

Let's be absolutely clear that veganism is not clean eating – and vice versa. Most people, although not everyone, choose to eat no (or less) animal produce for ethical reasons. It just so happens that the vegan way of eating is generally pretty healthy because it concentrates on simple wholefoods, but it's perfectly possible to enjoy indulgent – and cruelty-free – treats as well. Just ask anyone who's tried vegan mac and cheese or the Kentucky Fried Cauliflower on page 131. And just because veganism is getting more popular by the day, that doesn't mean that it's a faddy diet. It's a considered change, a social shift.

It's definitely a nice feeling to know that the food on your plate hasn't caused any harm or suffering, but there's nothing worthy about these recipes and the emphasis is always on taste and texture. Of course, there's merit in eating simple and unprocessed foods most of the time, but life is all about balance and nothing you eat is 'bad' or 'unclean'.

I'll be completely honest: I initially thought that eating a vegan diet would force me to stop eating 'bad' foods and that eliminating rich and decadent foods would make me thinner. Well, reader, it did, but I wasn't happy. Yes, I could fit into a certain size of jeans for the first time in my life, but I was hungry all the time and my periods stopped for a year. It seems that I, like many others, fell into the clean eating trap.

It's hardly surprising given that I grew up with various diets vomited up at me by the media. We could choose from low carb, no carbs, low fat, low calorie, the cabbage soup diet, the Zone Diet, Slimfast, and many more – and we swallowed them all. Meanwhile, junk food was being shoved in my face by an avalanche of adverts for Club biscuits, Pringles and Sunny Delight. Nowadays sugar is the devil and gluten is supposedly bad for us.

I remember my mum's magazines telling me that I could lose weight and have the perfect body by eating this or cutting out that – and they're still peddling this junk. At the same time, a new and delicious role model appeared in the shape of Nigella Lawson – and she told us that no foods were off limits. At the time, I was a bit confused but I learned as I got older that she wasn't saying that we should eat puddings and pies all day every day but that it's completely fine to enjoy a little bit of what you fancy.

After turning vegan, I gradually realised that woman cannot live on vegetables alone and I started eating a wider variety of foods – and that now includes vegan cheese toasties. It may have taken me over thirty years but I've finally found that balance. I've discovered my true appetite for eating – and life.

I think it's very important to listen to your body and what it's trying to tell you. Sometimes, you'll really want or need (the two aren't always separate entities) that chocolate cake, hot buttered toast slathered in jam or a pillowy mound of mashed potatoes. That's OK. There might be other days when you genuinely crave broccoli or avocado – and even though these are full of nutrients, you shouldn't eat too many of these either. As my mum has always said: too much of anything is bad for you. There are no shoulds and shouldn'ts when it comes to food, although you really shouldn't feel guilty about eating anything – easier said than done, I know. But it's healthy to indulge once in a while (hell, even on a regular basis if it makes you feel good), although if it makes you feel unhappy or uncomfortable, please talk to someone about it as you may need a little help with your relationship with food.

Difficult as it may sound, we need to listen to our bodies. For me, wellness means being kind to yourself and doing what works for you and your body. I hope that this book can help you find balance and that you, like me, will learn to enjoy food and cooking.

How to use this book

In this book, you'll find that flavour always comes first; the fact that most of these simple and delicious dishes are pretty nourishing is a bonus. This is a balanced approach to eating and I don't divide the recipes into 'healthy' or 'unhealthy' – because there simply is no such thing. Some of the dishes are more decadent and are designed to be enjoyed as a treat, while others, although still hearty, are things you might eat on a more regular basis.

The book is divided into four sections:

1. The working week: quick and easy breakfasts, lunches and dinners
2. Something for the weekend: lazy brunches, lunches and meals for friends and family
3. High days and holidays: dishes for special occasions
4. Comfort food and childhood favourites: think cawl, lasagne and chocolate brownies

You can afford to be a bit rough and ready with these recipes because, after all, no two dishes will ever yield exactly the same results. I'm always tweaking recipes (rule breaker that I am) but when it comes to baking, a precise art, I find that it's best to stick to the guidelines.

Eating well – what does it mean?

There's an overwhelming amount of advice out there about what eating well is – and isn't. I'm not a nutritionist but I know how to eat a balanced diet and that's what most of us can aim to do. I think pretty much every food writer or nutritionist has referenced Michael Pollan, who says that to be healthy, we must simply 'Eat food. Not too much. Mostly plants'.

He's right, but getting the balance right can be difficult at times. It seems that we live in a world of extremes. On one end of the spectrum, obesity looms large and at the other we are tangled up in a dangerous web of clean eating, fad diets and an obsession with eating only 'healthy' foods – which is also known as orthorexia. Don't believe the myth that all vegans have Insta-bodies (I don't) and only eat kale and avocado (I certainly don't). It's all about balance and if you deny yourself treats, you'll only crave them more.

Getting your nutrients

It's important to eat a varied diet when you decide to eat vegan. Despite what your mother says, you'd be surprised by how little protein we actually need and how it can be found in a number of vegetables, beans and pulses. The same goes for iron, calcium and healthy fats. Nutrients can be found in the most surprising of places; for example, did you know that black treacle is a good source of calcium and iron?

Here's the lowdown on what everyone (not only vegans) needs to be healthy.

Vitamin A

This helps your immune system fight illness and infection, keeps your skin healthy and helps you see in the dark – yes, really! Most sources come from animal products but you can get your daily dose by eating carrots, sweet potatoes, red peppers, green leafy vegetables, mango and apricots as these contain beta-carotene which the body can turn into vitamin A. Men need 0.7mg of vitamin A per day and women need 0.6mg – that could be half a sweet potato or 50g (two large handfuls) of kale.

Vitamin B

There are many different types of vitamin B and your body uses these to release energy, maintain a healthy nervous system and keep your skin looking bright. It's possible to get all the different types from a vegan diet although B12 can be tricky as it's only found naturally in foods from animal sources. You can get some from fortified breakfast cereals and soya drinks and Marmite (if you like it) but a vitamin B12 supplement may be needed as a lack of it could lead to vitamin B12 deficiency and anaemia.

Vitamin C

This helps to protect cells, maintains healthy skin, blood vessels, bones and cartilage and helps with wound healing. Luckily for vegans, it can be found in a wide variety of fruits and vegetables, including oranges and orange juice, red and green peppers, strawberries, blackcurrants, broccoli, Brussels sprouts and potatoes. Adults need 40mg of vitamin C a day, which could be a small orange, a few broccoli florets or a medium-sized potato.

Vitamin D

The body needs vitamin D to regulate the amount of calcium and phosphate in the body as these keep bones, teeth and muscles healthy. Most sources of vitamin D are animal-based but vegans get some of it from exposure to summer sunshine, fortified fat spreads, breakfast cereals and unsweetened soya drinks (with vitamin D added) and supplements. Check the label to make sure that the vitamin D used in a product is not of animal origin. Adults need 10mcg of vitamin D a day and, from about late March/early April to the end of September, the majority of people in the UK should be able to get all the vitamin D they need from sunlight on their skin.

Vitamin E

This helps maintain healthy skin and eyes, and strengthen the body's natural defence against illness and infection. Good sources include plant oils – such as soya, corn and olive oil, nuts and seeds – and wheatgerm, which is found in cereals and cereal products. Any vitamin E your body doesn't need immediately is stored for future use, so you don't need it in your diet every day. Men need 4mg of vitamin E a day, while women need 3mg, and you can get this from a handful of almonds or a small avocado.

Vitamin K

Vitamin K is needed for blood clotting as it helps wounds heal properly and it also helps to keep bones healthy. It's found in green leafy vegetables, vegetable oils and cereal grains. Adults need approximately 1mcg a day of vitamin K for each kilogram of their body weight. Adults need approximately 1mcg a day of vitamin K for each kilogram of their body weight.

For example, someone who weighs 65kg would need 65mcg a day of vitamin K, or a serving of broccoli or romaine lettuce. You should be able to get all the vitamin K you need by eating a varied and balanced diet and any vitamin K your body doesn't need immediately is stored in the liver for future use, so you don't need it every day.

Calcium

We need this for strong and healthy bones and teeth, and contrary to popular belief, it's not only found in dairy. Good sources of calcium for vegans include fortified, unsweetened soya, rice and oat drinks, tofu, sesame seeds and tahini, pulses, brown and white bread (in the UK, calcium is added to white and brown flour by law) and dried fruit, such as raisins, prunes, figs and dried apricots. Adults need 700mg of calcium a day. You'll find 107mg of calcium in eight dried figs, 200mg in half a tin of black beans, 861mg in half a 400g block of tofu, and even 50mg in 10g of black treacle.

Iron

Iron is essential for the production of red blood cells and even if you don't eat meat, you can enjoy a diet that's high in iron. Good sources include pulses, wholemeal bread and flour, breakfast cereals fortified with iron, dark green leafy vegetables, such as watercress, broccoli and spring greens, nuts, and dried fruits such as apricots, prunes and figs, and even treacle. Women over 50 and men need 8.7mg of iron a day, while women aged between 19 and 50 will need 14.8mg a day. A serving of chickpeas will provide 12.5mg of iron, while a bowl of iron-fortified cereal can contain as much as 18mg.

Fibre

Fibre is an important part of a healthy balanced diet as it can help prevent heart disease, diabetes, weight gain and some cancers, and can also improve digestive health. On average, most people in the UK only get about 18g of fibre a day when we should aim for at least 30g. Fortunately for vegans, fibre is found only in foods that come from plants. There are two types of fibre: soluble and insoluble. Soluble fibre dissolves in the water in your digestive system, can reduce the amount of cholesterol in your blood and stops you getting constipated. Good sources of soluble fibre are oats, barley, rye, fruit, root vegetables and golden linseeds. Insoluble fibre doesn't dissolve in water and passes through your gut without being broken down, helping other foods move through your digestive system. It can be found in wholemeal bread, bran, cereals and nuts and most seeds and should make up around a quarter of your daily fibre intake.

Protein

We need protein so that the body can grow and repair itself. Men between 19 and 50 years old need 55.5g of protein a day while women between 19 and 50 years old need 45g and elderly people need around 53g. Good vegan sources include beans, frozen peas, seeds and nuts, tahini, tofu, chickpeas and lentils; in fact, just three tablespoons of cooked lentils provides 9g of protein. A serving of beans contains as much protein as 90g of grilled steak and 100g of tofu has about 23.5g.

Fats

Not all fat is bad and a small amount of it is an essential part of a healthy, balanced diet as it helps the body absorb vitamins A, D and E. As part of a healthy diet, we should try to cut down on foods and drinks high in saturated fats and trans fats, such as butter, cakes, bacon and milkshakes, and replace some of them with unsaturated fats which are found primarily in oils from plants and fish.

Monounsaturated fats help protect our hearts by maintaining levels of good cholesterol, and can be found in olive oil, rapeseed oil and their spreads, avocados and some nuts, such as almonds, brazils and peanuts.

Polyunsaturated fats can help lower the level of bad cholesterol and there are two main types: omega-3 and omega-6. Vegan sources of omega-3 include flaxseed (linseed) oil, rapeseed oil, soya-based foods, such as tofu, and walnuts. Omega-6 fats are found in vegetable oils, like rapeseed, corn, sunflower and some nuts.

Carbohydrates

Carbs are not the enemy! They play an important part in our diet and we should get around half our calorie intake from them because their sugars and starches help provide the body with energy and dietary fibre, and eating too few carbs can lead to constipation. It can also cause low blood sugar levels, which can make you feel weak or light headed.

You should try to eat mainly complex carbohydrates containing starch which is found in cereals, grains, bread, flour, pasta, rice, some fruit and vegetables and breakfast cereal. These give the body important vitamins and minerals such as calcium, iron and B vitamins. Simple carbs, which are found in sugary foods and drinks, offer little nutritional value, are high in calories and cause blood sugar levels to rise and then fall rapidly, leaving you hungry and quite often cranky.

Getting started...

Eating and cooking the vegan way can seem like a minefield but it's actually very simple once you know how – and a lot cheaper because buying meat is expensive. Here's a general guide to everything you need to get started in your vegan kitchen.

Kitting out your kitchen

I've divided this into what you what you'll need in your cupboard, fruit bowl, fridge and freezer.

Cupboard

Grains: brown rice, white rice, quinoa, bulgur wheat, buckwheat, pearl barley, couscous, polenta, oats

Dry pasta and noodles: spaghetti, penne, orzo, egg-free lasagne sheets, rice noodles, wholewheat noodles

Vegetables: potatoes, sweet potatoes, onions

Tins, jars, packets and tubes: tomatoes (chopped and whole), sundried tomatoes, tomato purée, sweetcorn, coconut milk, dried mushrooms, stock powder or cubes, gravy granules, nutritional yeast flakes, microwave rice, jackfruit, black and green olives, capers, Marmite, peanut butter

Beans and lentils: aduki beans, black beans, borlotti beans, butter beans, cannellini beans, chickpeas, haricot beans, kidney beans, pinto beans, green lentils, puy lentils, red split lentils

Nuts and seeds: whole almonds, flaked almonds, walnuts, pecans, cashews, peanuts (unsalted), Brazil nuts, pistachios, pine nuts, pumpkin seeds, sunflower seeds, sesame seeds, flaxseed (or linseed), chia seeds

Dried herbs: basil, bay leaves, thyme, marjoram, oregano, rosemary, saffron, sage, tarragon

Spices: allspice, caraway seeds, celery salt, Chinese five spice, cinnamon (ground and sticks), cumin (ground and seeds), curry powder, dried red chilli flakes, coriander (ground and seeds), fennel seeds, ground ginger, garam masala, paprika, smoked paprika, turmeric, yellow and black mustard seeds, sea salt, black peppercorns, whole nutmeg, chilli powder, ras el hanout, sumac

Sweet stuff: agave honey, maple syrup, brown sugar, caster sugar, treacle, dried fruit, cocoa powder, strawberry jam, dark chocolate, vanilla essence, almond extract, vegan digestive biscuits

For baking: plain flour, self-raising flour, bicarbonate soda, baking powder, sugar, ready-roll pastry, icing sugar

Oils and vinegars: olive oil, extra virgin olive oil; coconut oil, rapeseed oil, sesame oil, vegetable or sunflower oil, balsamic vinegar, white wine vinegar, apple cider vinegar

Sauces: tabasco sauce, tomato ketchup, mustard, soy sauce, miso paste, harissa paste, mango chutney, curry paste, Thai green curry paste (make sure to choose a vegan version)

The fruit bowl

It's not just for fruit. Keep some of your vegetables at room temperature for optimal flavour.

Apples, oranges, bananas, pink grapefruit, tomatoes, peppers, avocados, aubergines, chillies, garlic, lemons and limes, root ginger

Fridge

Unwaxed lemons and limes (these go off more quickly if you leave them in the fruit bowl), cucumber, salad leaves, celery, carrots, mushrooms, broccoli, cauliflower

Fresh herbs like flat leaf parsley, rosemary, thyme, mint, basil, sage and coriander – or grow your own on the windowsill. You can keep herbs and greens for longer by rolling them up in damp paper towels and placing them in freezer bags with the seals left slightly open.

Tofu
Vegan margarine
Vegan cheese
Vegan yogurt
Plant milk (my favourite is oat milk but soya, rice, almond, cashew, hazelnut etc. are all good choices)
Vegan mayonnaise

Freezer

Frozen peas
Frozen sweetcorn
Frozen berries
Homemade stock
Leftovers!
Remember that food should only be defrosted once

A guide to shopping

You might think that veganism is only for well-off lefties but it's not a middle-class fad; it's actually really accessible for those of us on a tight budget.

Once your kitchen is stocked, shopping shouldn't be expensive. Seasonal fruit and vegetables are cheap and plentiful, and beans, pulses, rice and other grains cost pennies. Meals like chilli, dhal and curry are tasty tummy fillers which, armed with a well-stocked cupboard, will cost you next nothing to make. You can buy big bags of pulses for next to nothing in all supermarkets – or even better, at your nearest Asian supermarket where they'll be even cheaper. Some pulses need soaking overnight so if that sounds like a faff just stock up on tins. Again, check out the international aisle at larger supermarkets as tins of chickpeas and other pulses are much cheaper there. Visit your local pound or bargain shops where you can often find things like quinoa, nuts, seeds and dried fruit at a fraction of the price you'd pay at the supermarket.

If you're shopping on a budget, visit your local greengrocer or supermarket as both will stock a range of cheap and plentiful produce. I haven't got into growing my vegetables yet (and at the moment, I live in a flat without a garden) but it's a very good way to get your nutrients on the cheap.

Seasonal produce

I don't want to be a bore (or a snob) about this but buying fruits and vegetables that are in season is much tastier and is better value for money. It's also kinder to the environment as it saves on air miles and is a good way to support British producers. Having said that, we must be realistic – it's not always possible to get something that's locally and organically grown (as lovely as that would be) and no one would begrudge you for using whatever fruit and vegetables you find in the shops. You won't catch me eating strawberries in February though – because they taste bloody horrible.

Here's a rough guide to what's in season and when.

Spring

Asparagus, broad beans, beetroot, purple sprouting broccoli, cauliflower, celeriac, chard, cherries, cucumber, gooseberries, kale, leeks, lettuce, mushrooms, onions, parsnips, pumpkin, radishes, rhubarb, spring greens, swede, turnips, samphire, sorrel, sugarsnap peas, watercress.

Summer

Asparagus, aubergine, broad beans, beetroot, broccoli, cauliflower, chicory, chillies, courgette, cucumber, fennel, garlic, green beans, kohlrabi, lettuce, mangetout, new potatoes, peas, peaches, radishes, raspberries, rhubarb, rocket, runner beans, samphire, shallots, sorrel, squash, strawberries, sugarsnap peas, sweetcorn, sweet peppers, tomatoes, watercress.

Autumn

Apples, aubergine, beetroot, blackberries, Brussels sprouts, broccoli, cauliflower, celeriac, chard, chicory, courgettes, cucumber, fennel, garlic, gooseberries, kale, kohlrabi, leeks, lettuce, mushrooms, new potatoes, parsnips, peas, pears, plums, pumpkin, radishes, rocket, runner beans, salsify, samphire, shallots, sorrel, squash, swede, sweet peppers, sweet potatoes, sweetcorn, tomatoes, turnips, watercress.

Winter

Beetroot, Brussels sprouts, broccoli, celeriac, chard, chestnuts, kale, leeks, mushrooms, okra, parsnips, peas, pears, pumpkin, radicchio, salsify, samphire, shallots, squash, swede, turnips.

All year round

Artichokes (globe and Jerusalem), avocados, bananas, cabbage, carrots, celery, pomegranates, potatoes, spinach, spring onions

Quick fixes

I'm going to let you in on a little secret: convenience food can be your friend. Being vegan doesn't have to be hard work, and if you're short of time and energy it makes sense to take shortcuts. I love cooking, but sometimes I don't want to chop or stir or fry or bake or roast – and I certainly don't want to wash up afterwards.

If you know what to look for, you'll find lots of quick tricks to help save you time. Those microwaveable pouches of rice and quinoa, for example, are a godsend. The Uncle Ben and Tilda ones are often reduced and the own brand versions can cost as little as 50p. If you don't have a microwave, you can heat the rice in a pan in less than five minutes. I also love frozen vegetables, shop-bought houmous and tinned pulses as they're all are pretty healthy and contain mainly natural ingredients.

Alcohol

You wouldn't think it but not all alcohol is created vegan thanks to added ingredients which are usually made from animal derivatives. Although wine is made predominately from grapes, the final 'fining' process often uses animal derivatives to latch onto any impurities in the wine, so that unwanted particles can be easily caught in the filters before bottling. White, rosé and sparkling wines typically use isinglass, which is derived from fish bladders, to make the end product clear and bright. Egg whites and milk protein are also often used in red wine to remove any bitter flavours. Some fortified wines, like port and sherry, sometimes have gelatine added. Not all wines will tell you this on the label, although most supermarkets sell own-brand vegan wine. You can also look online to find out if your favourite brand is safe to drink. Be aware that organic does not always mean plant-based, so always check if you're unsure.

Many mainstream lager brands are free from animal products but real ale can often contain isinglass so it's worth checking the label or looking online. The vast majority of ciders are not vegan friendly as some of the most popular brands incorporate gelatine into their manufacturing.

Spirits are mostly safe to drink, and the most popular and widely-used spirit brands are suitable, although some imported vodkas are filtered with charred animal bones as part of the sugar-refining process. Cream-based liquors often contain dairy products (although you can now get vegan Baileys!) and milk, cream and even eggs can also make an appearance in cocktails – and remember that a Bloody Mary cocktail is not vegan-friendly as Worcester sauce contains anchovies, so ask your bartender to leave it out or to use HP sauce instead.

Tools and gadgets

You'll need a few kitchen essentials for cooking simple – and more elaborate – meals. With all of these, buy the best you can afford.

Knives – you'll need a fairly large chef's knife (about 17.5-20cm/7-8 inches), a smaller knife (15cm/6 inches) and a bread knife. It's useful to have a knife sharpener, too.
Chopping boards
A box grater
Kitchen tongs
Saucepans – you'll need small, medium and large ones
Frying pans – buy non-stick
A casserole – buy a flame and heatproof one if you can so that it can go on the hob and in the oven
Roasting and baking trays
A sieve
A silicone whisk
A vegetable peeler
Mixing bowls
Pestle and mortar
Cake tins (buy non-stick if you can, so that you don't have to grease them)
Food processor – this isn't essential but it will save you time in the kitchen
Hand blender – if you can't afford a food processor or have little room in your kitchen, get one of these: they're inexpensive and are great for blending soups and sauces
Weighing scales – Again, these aren't essential if you're a fairly experienced cook as you can generally judge how much of the ingredients you need to use, but you will need them for baking as precision is key. I find that digital scales are always more accurate.

Oven temperatures

All ovens are different so when following a recipe, you may find that you will need to adjust times and temperatures ever so slightly. I prefer to use an electric oven as the heat is distributed more evenly through the oven meaning that cooking is easier – and that's what I've used for all of the recipes in this book, so if you have a gas or electric fan oven, use this rough guide to oven temperatures when cooking.

	Electricity °C	Electricity (fan) °C	Gas mark
Very cool	110	90	¼
	120	100	¼
Cool	140	120	1
	150	130	2
Moderate	160	140	3
	180	160	4
Moderately hot	190	170	5
	200	180	6
Hot	220	200	7
	230	210	8
Very hot	240	220	9

How to…

Here's my guide to (probably) some of the most Googled questions about cooking certain things. If you're a seasoned cook, you'll know all of this, but if you don't, here's how I make some of the kitchen classics.

Make vegetable stock

This is absolutely non-essential, as you can buy perfectly good vegan stock cubes and powder, but it's a lot cheaper to make your own and you can store it in the freezer and use it when you need it. It's also a good way to use up vegetable peelings, provided that they were washed beforehand.

You'll need:
1 onion, peeled and roughly chopped
1 carrot, peeled and roughly chopped
2 celery stalks, sliced
2 bay leaves
1-2 sprigs of thyme (or 1 tsp dried – or whichever herb you prefer)
Salt and pepper

Put all the ingredients into a saucepan and cover with water. Bring up to the boil and simmer very gently for 30 minutes. Strain through a sieve and chill or freeze once cool. Stock will keep in the fridge for up to two days but if you want to keep it for longer, pour into ice cube trays and freeze.

Cook rice

It took me a little while to get to grips with rice and, from chatting to friends, it seems that I'm not the only one who finds it tricky. Here's a failsafe method for cooking rice. You'll need between 60g and 100g of rice per person and if in doubt, cook extra because it's better to have too much than too little.

Bring a large pan of salted water to the boil and while it heats up, tip the rice into a sieve and run under the cold tap to remove any starch, then leave to drain. Tip the rice into the boiling water and cook until just tender – usually this will take about 20 minutes, although brown rice will take longer, so check the packet instructions. Drain thoroughly. If you're not serving it immediately, tip the drained rice back into the saucepan and cover with a lid to keep it warm.

Cook pasta

Take a large pan (you'll need around 100g dried pasta per person) and fill it two-thirds full with water and place on a high heat. Add a generous pinch of salt and when the water has come to a boil, tip in the pasta and cook for 8-10 minutes, or according to packet instructions. Stir once or twice to prevent it from sticking to the pan. It's much better to have it slightly 'al dente' (firm and 'to the bite') than overcooked and soggy so take a piece or strand from the pan and bite into it to test it. When it's ready, drain well and serve immediately.

Make mashed potatoes

Believe it or not, it's possible to make the creamiest of mashed potatoes without using dairy. Here's how:

Take your potatoes (you'll need floury ones so use King Edwards or something similar) and scrub or peel them – it's fine to leave the skins on. Place in a large pan and cover with water and a pinch of salt and bring to the boil. Boil for about 20 minutes or until tender – test with a fork or the tip of a sharp knife. Drain and return to the pan. Now, you can add either vegan margarine or olive oil (be generous), some salt and pepper, and if you like, a little plant milk. Mash with a potato masher until smooth and as lump-free as possible, adding more milk if you want a creamier consistency. Warm over a low heat, stirring constantly and serve.

Make your own curry paste

You can, of course, buy this in a jar (check the label to make sure it's vegan-friendly) but making your own curry paste takes no time at all. If you haven't got a food processor or blender, just cut the ingredients into smaller pieces and bash together in a pestle and mortar.

You'll need:
1 red onion, cut into chunks
2–3 red chillies, stalks removed and cut into three
50g fresh ginger, peeled and cut into chunks
2 garlic cloves, peeled and halved
1 tsp ground turmeric
1 tsp ground coriander
½ tsp ground cinnamon
1 tsp sea salt flakes

Put the onion, chillies, ginger, garlic, turmeric, ground coriander, cinnamon and salt into a food processor and blend to a paste, or use a stick blender and a bowl.

Cook vegetables

Without stating the obvious or being too patronising, here's a quick guide to boiling or steaming, frying or stir-frying and roasting vegetables.

Boiling or steaming

Half fill a saucepan with water, add a pinch of salt and bring to the boil. Place the prepared vegetables into the water and boil. If steaming, add the steamer part, place the prepared vegetables into that and cover with a lid.

Stir-frying

The secret to good stir frying is not to put too much in the wok at once, because if you do, the vegetables will sweat instead of frying. Heat your wok until it's really hot. Add a splash of oil – it should start to smoke – then add your vegetables. Flip

occasionally with a wooden spoon and after a minute or two, the vegetables should have begun to soften. Add soy sauce and lemon or lime juice, and sesame oil, if you like, and stir in. Cook for another 2 minutes or so and serve.

Roasting

If all else fails and you have time to do one thing on a Sunday, roast a big tray of vegetables to last you throughout the week. Preheat the oven to 200C, cut the vegetables in half or into chunks and spread them out onto a baking dish or sheet, making sure that they're not crowded as this will steam them instead of roasting them. Use about two tablespoons of oil and toss the vegetables with your hands to rub it in and make sure they're evenly coated. Season with salt and pepper and cook according to the following guide.

Vegetable	Goes well with	Roast for...
Cauliflower	Olive oil, cumin, cinnamon, lemon juice	25 minutes
Tendersteam broccoli	Sesame oil, chilli powder, lime juice	20 minutes
Potatoes	Olive or vegetable oil, rosemary or thyme, lemon juice	Parboil for 10 minutes then roast for 45-60 minutes
Tomatoes	Olive oil, salt, thyme or sage	15 minutes
Carrots	Sesame oil, orange juice, cinnamon	25 minutes
Beetroot	Olive oil, orange juice	30-40 minutes
Brussels sprouts	Olive oil, maple syrup, pecans, cinammon	30 minutes
Onions	Olive oil, thyme	15-20 minutes
Butternut squash and pumpkin	Olive oil, cinnamon	45-60 minutes
Aubergine	Sesame oil, soy sauce, lime juice	15-20 minutes
Courgette	Olive oil, lemon, flaked almonds	10-15 minutes
Peppers	Olive oil, garlic	15-20 minutes

My kitchen commandments

Everyone has their own set of rules for the kitchen and here are my simple tips to help make things easier (and taste better) when you're cooking.

1. Be organised! Yes, it's boring but be prepared to prep because it'll save you a lot of time and unnecessary stress. Before cooking, make sure that your kitchen surfaces are clear and get out all the ingredients and equipment you need for the recipe. Peel and chop all your vegetables before you start cooking and keep a pot for vegetable peelings so that you don't have to run back and forth to the bin.

2. Don't waste food. Keep those peelings for stock, throw leftover vegetables into soup or a stir-fry (or roast), and use brown bananas as a sweetener in cakes – and if necessary, you can freeze them and use at a later date.

3. Use things at room temperature so that they take less time to cook. Fruit and vegetables cold from the fridge don't taste of much so take them out at least an hour before eating or cooking.

4. Learn to love batch cooking. If you can spare a couple of hours on a Sunday afternoon or evening, you can make a lot of your meals for the week ahead which will save you a lot of time and energy.

5. If you buy salad leaves in a plastic bag, they'll soon turn to mulch. Take them out and keep in a covered bowl or Tupperware box in the fridge.

6. Whatever you do, don't wash your mushrooms – unless you want slimy, watery slugs, that is. Simply remove any dirt with some kitchen roll.

7. Fat is flavour so don't fear it. Don't skimp on olive oil or nuts or avocados because they add taste and texture – plus they're all good for you. If you're really bothered about extra calories, you can always have something lighter for your next meal.

8. Don't use any more pots, pans or utensils than necessary (think of the washing up) and tidy up as you go along.

9. Buy the best ingredients you can afford because it can really make a difference to the taste of your cooking. Having said that, cheap tinned tomatoes and pulses taste exactly the same as more expensive versions.

10. Finally, enjoy! Cooking is fun and eating is fun. Even if things go wrong in the kitchen (because, sometimes, they do), you can almost always save a dish and you might even make it better – after all cooking is all about invention and creativity. It's only a meal, so don't stress.

Eating out

Cutting out animal products doesn't mean you automatically lose your taste buds, although I think a few restaurant chefs need to be told this… no, I don't want a bland butternut squash risotto with zero seasoning, thank you very much. Thankfully, in the past year or two, it's become a lot easier for vegans to eat at restaurants. Most of the chains offer a special menu and it's always worth checking out the independent restaurants in your town or city. Never be afraid to order off menu. Have a quick chat with your waiter or waitress (or if you can, call the restaurant in advance) and the kitchen should be able to make something for you – or perhaps veganise an existing veggie dish. Anywhere worth its salt will be willing to do this. Yes, you will sometimes resent paying for food that is bland and unimaginative, but at the end of the day you will sometimes have to eat at a restaurant chosen by someone else, so enjoy the company – and offer to choose where you go next time.

If you're grabbing lunch on the go, most chain cafes and supermarkets offer something for vegans, too. If there really is nothing suitable to eat, grab some fruit or a plain salad and a little bag of nuts and seeds for sustenance. It's boring but it'll keep you going until you can eat something decent.

The recipes

The working week

Life's busy so with that in mind, I've put together this collection of recipes, which are all quick and easy to make but still full of flavour, and will give you the sustenance you need to make it through to the weekend. I've divided these recipes into breakfast, lunch and dinner but they can all be enjoyed at any time of the day. Anything that you make for dinner can also be used as leftovers for lunch the following day. Every one of them can be made in around 30 minutes and I've included little shortcuts in most of them, so that they take even less time to go from pan to plate.

Brisk breakfasts

It's true what they say: breakfast is the most important meal of the day. After sleeping all night, your body will be running on empty and in need of fuel. I always wake up hungry but some people can't face eating first thing. If that's you, try to have something small, even if it's just a smoothie or a bowl of cereal. These brisk breakfasts take no time at all to make in the morning and most can be made the night before and eaten on the go or when you get to work.

Lovely lunches

Whether you work from home, at an office or somewhere else, you need a good lunch to keep you going. If I ever forget to eat during the day (and this only happens when I'm really busy), I get seriously cranky. Choose something quick to eat that's filling and nutritious and while I can't promise that it'll make your day perfect, it will make it that little bit easier. These lovely lunches can all be made in advance so that you can take them to the office or can be quickly assembled in the kitchen.

Simple suppers

When you slither through the door after another busy day, often the last thing you want to do is cook. Take half an hour to put something together and I promise you won't regret it. These simple suppers are exactly that and they're hearty and healthy, too.

Jolly juice

A sure-fire way to get your vitamin C. Even if you don't have a juicer, you can use a food processor to make this fresh juice in under ten minutes – or you can even make it and chill overnight. Tweak this to your liking – if you want a little more sweetness, you can add an apple or banana. I sometimes add a little sliced red chilli if I really need some pep or if I've got the sniffles – but I realise this isn't to everyone's liking!

Under 10 minutes | Serves 1

Ingredients

– 1 large orange
– Half a large pink grapefruit
– 1 medium carrot, scrubbed or peeled
– 1-2 stalks celery, ends removed
– 1 tsp fresh ginger, peeled
– 100-150ml water

If you're using a juicer, roughly chop the carrot and celery, add the orange and grapefruit juice and the ginger and blend. If you're using a food processor, you'll need to dice the carrot, celery and ginger as finely as you can. Place this in the food processor with a little of the water and pulse on a high setting for about a minute. Now add the orange and grapefruit juice and the rest of the water and pulse again, for about a minute. You can either drink this juice with the pulp (you may need to use a straw!) or if you want a smoother consistency, simply strain through a sieve, pushing down with a wooden spoon so that you get as much juice as possible. Don't throw away the pulp! It may sound frugal but it's a shame to waste such goodness and you can pop it into stock, marinades, dressings or sauces. Or add it to a mashed avocado and spread on toast or put it in a sandwich with crunchy peanut butter and thinly sliced cucumber.

The perfect porridge

Goldilocks knew her stuff when it came to porridge: it needs to be *just* right. Too much liquid makes it sloppy, while too little can mean that you end up with an almost biscuit-like texture – I should know, that's how I used to make it until someone showed me how.

Making porridge is a piece of cake once you get the hang of it, and if you know you're going to be in a rush, you can make overnight oats: just place all your ingredients in a bowl, leave in the fridge overnight and heat in on the hob or microwave come the morning.

5 minutes | Serves 1

Ingredients

– 4 tbsp oats
– Half a mugful of oat or plant milk – or water

Simply place the oats and liquid, plus whatever fruit you're using, into a saucepan and cook on a low heat for 3-4 minutes, stirring continuously. Serve in a bowl and top with nuts, cinnamon or ginger, and a sprinkling of brown sugar or maple syrup.

The number of porridge toppings are limitless. Try these flavour combinations:

– Fresh or frozen berries, a tablespoon of maple syrup and a handful of flaked almonds
– Mashed banana, a tablespoon of peanut butter, cocoa powder and cinnamon
– Dried fruit and a squeeze of orange juice, topped with a tablespoon of tahini
– Fresh or tinned peaches with a dash of vanilla essence and a handful of crushed pistachios
– Stewed or tinned rhubarb and grated apple with a teaspoon of fresh or ground ginger, a smattering of brown sugar and a dollop of tahini
– Sliced pear, a handful of pecans, a tablespoon of maple syrup and cinnamon
– Pear or apple with grated carrot, fresh or ground ginger and a handful of walnuts and raisins

Super smoothie

This is one sweet way to start the day and is super easy to make. The oats and peanut butter turn this into a smoothie with substance that should keep you full until lunchtime. The spinach is optional but I promise that, if you do include it, you won't notice that it's there. One for the vegetable avoiders out there, perhaps.

5 minutes | Serves 1

Ingredients

– 200ml oat milk
– 1 medium banana
– 2 handfuls of fresh or frozen berries
– 2 handfuls of spinach (optional)
– 2 tbsp oats
– 1 tbsp peanut butter
– 1 tsp ground cinnamon
– ½ tsp ground ginger

This is easy peasy. Put everything in a blender and pulse for a minute or less. Pour into a glass – or a bottle if you're planning to drink this on the move.

Granola

When I'm in a rush, granola is my 'go to' breakfast because it requires very little preparation and I can eat it quickly before heading out of the door. This is very easy to make and costs a lot less than the kind you'd buy at the supermarket. It's not too sugar laden and the protein in the nuts and seeds should keep you full until lunchtime.

As a kid, I ate my cereal dry because I've never liked cow's milk. Nowadays, I eat my granola with fresh or frozen fruit and some plant milk or coconut yogurt – and I've also been known to eat a few handfuls while I'm waiting for dinner to cook.

30-35 minutes | Makes enough for 5-6 servings

Ingredients

– 200g jumbo oats
– 100g mixed nuts like walnuts and pecans, chopped roughly
– 50g flaked almonds
– 100g dried apricots, chopped (use scissors if it's easier)
– 50g pumpkin seeds
– 3 tbsp olive oil
– 2 tbsp maple syrup
– 1 tsp almond essence
– 1 tsp cinnamon
– The juice of one large orange

Preheat the oven to 180C. In a large bowl, mix together all the ingredients then spread evenly onto a large baking tray (you may need to use two) and make sure that the mixture is spread out so that it cooks evenly. Place on the middle shelf of the oven and bake for 20-25 minutes or until the nuts are toasted but not burned. Allow to cool then serve with plant milk, vegan yogurt or on its own. Store in an airtight container and eat within 4-5 days.

God's butter
(pea and avocado spread)

I've heard a few people refer to avocados as 'God's butter' and I can see why. These green goddesses are deliciously creamy and packed with vitamins and healthy fats. This little twist on your average avocado on toast is full of fresh flavours, which will pep you up nicely for the day ahead. The peas are a great way to get some protein first thing, too.

5-10 minutes | Serves 2

Ingredients

– 150g frozen peas or petit pois
– 1 medium avocado (ripe)
– The juice of half a lime
– ½ a red chilli, finely sliced
– 1 tsp fresh ginger, peeled and finely chopped
– 2-3 mint leaves, finely chopped
– 1 tbsp tahini

Boil or steam the peas for 2-3 minutes, then drain and rinse with cold water. In a bowl, use a fork or potato masher to mash the avocado with the chilli, ginger and mint, then add the peas and continue mashing. Stir through the tahini and lime juice and serve on toast.

Berry booster

I know what you're thinking: who eats vegetables first thing in the morning? Plenty of people across the world, actually. This savoury breakfast is light enough to stomach (even if you have an early start, plus you can make it the night before) and gives a powerful punch of protein. The berries add a bit of sweetness and lots of vitamin C and you get calcium and zinc from the green vegetables. If your tahini is a little too thick you can whisk it up with a drop or two of water so that it's easier to drizzle.

10 minutes | Serves 2

Ingredients

– 1 x 400g can chickpeas, rinsed and drained
– 100g frozen berries
– Broccoli (or other green vegetables), as much or as little as you like
– 3-4 handfuls of kale or spinach
– 2 tsp tahini, at room temperature
– 1 tsp cinnamon
– 2 tsp pumpkin or sunflower seeds

Boil or steam the broccoli for 5 minutes. Heat the chickpeas and frozen berries in a pan and stir through the kale, allowing it to gently wilt. Serve in bowls with a drizzle of tahini, cinnamon and seeds.

Cheery choco-nut spread

We didn't often have Nutella as kids but when we did, it didn't last long. The shop-bought stuff isn't often vegan so when I'm feeling indulgent, I make my own. This is easy to make and tastes even better than the one you get in a jar. It's more suited to a grown-up palate as it's not super sweet so if you're making it for little ones, add more maple syrup or 100g brown sugar. This is best slathered onto thick white toast – or you can swirl it into porridge. Add a sliced banana if you want to get one of your five a day.

30 minutes | Makes enough for one medium-sized jar

Ingredients

– 200g hazelnuts
– 150ml plant milk
– 50ml olive oil
– 6 tbsp cocoa powder
– 4-5 tbsp maple syrup
– 2 tsp ground cinnamon
– 2 tsp vanilla extract
– Pinch of salt

Preheat the oven to 170C, then spread the hazelnuts onto a baking sheet and roast for 15 minutes until brown. Set aside to cool, then rub together in your hands to remove the loose skins – don't worry if some are still left on. In batches, place the hazelnuts in a food processor and pulse on the lowest setting for at least 2-3 minutes to get a fine consistency. When you have blended all the nuts, gradually add the other ingredients and pulse – you may have to scrape the sides of the food processor with a wooden spoon or spatula to get a smoother consistency. Add more maple syrup or cocoa powder, depending on how sweet you want it to be. When you're happy with the consistency, spoon into a jar. This should keep for about a week, depending on how much of a chocolate fiend you are…

Portable pot noodle

I've never eaten a proper pot noodle – it just doesn't appeal to me, because I imagine it would taste like chip shop curry sauce, one of the few things I really dislike. You can make a pretty fresh tasting and healthy one though, and the best thing is that you can make it in advance, then 'cook' it by pouring over boiling water. Use whatever veg you have in the fridge. I like dried mushrooms for their intense flavour but the fresh kind work well, too. Adjust the flavouring depending on how much soy sauce and spice you like – I tend to use a lot.

15 minutes | Serves 1

Ingredients

– 1 'nest' (or 50g) wholewheat or rice noodles
– ½ a red pepper, finely sliced
– ½ a carrot, peeled and sliced into matchsticks
– 1 stalk celery, ends removed and finely diced
– 10g dried mushrooms
– A small handful of curly kale
– 2 large handfuls of frozen peas
– 2-3 tsp sweet chilli or sriracha sauce
– 1-2 tsp vegetable stock powder
– 1 tsp ginger, peeled and chopped
– 1 tbsp soy sauce
– The juice of half a lime
– A handful of cashew nuts
– A handful of sliced red chilli (optional)

In a medium-sized heatproof jar or mug, press down the noodles, breaking them up a little. Now, top with the vegetables, then add the chilli sauce, soy sauce, stock powder and ginger. If you're planning to eat this later, pop on a lid and put it in your bag. When you're ready to eat it, simply boil the kettle and pour over the boiling water (about 250-300ml, or enough to cover the ingredients) and leave to stand for 10-12 minutes. Squeeze over the lime juice and top with the nuts and chilli, plus some more soy sauce, if you like.

Coronation chickpeas

Coronation chicken was a bit of a novelty growing up. It wasn't something we'd ever eat at home but sometimes I'd spot it as part of the buffet at a birthday party and I became quite enamoured with the stuff. As the years went by I forgot all about it – until one of my favourite sandwich shops introduced a version made with chickpeas and I was instantly hooked again.

As the name suggests, it was created in 1953 for a banquet to celebrate the coronation of Elizabeth II. The amalgamation of Anglo-Indian flavours offered a bit of exoticism to post-war Britain and it soon became a classic. This vegan version is sweetly spicy and creamy but not too heavy on the tummy. Great as part of a party spread or for an extra special sandwich filling – and it's nice piled onto a steaming baked potato, too.

5-10 minutes | Makes enough for 2-3 sandwiches

Ingredients

– 1 x 400g can chickpeas, rinsed and drained
– ½ a red pepper diced
– 2 tbsp vegan mayonnaise, plus extra for spreading
– 1½ tsp medium curry powder
– ½ tsp ground cumin
– 50g sultanas or raisins
– 50g flaked almonds (optional)
– 2 heaped tsp mango chutney, plus extra for spreading
– The juice of half a lemon

In a bowl, mix together all the ingredients. Take a slice of bread and spread over the chickpea mixture, then top with spinach leaves and thinly sliced cucumber. On another slice of bread, spread over a little mayonnaise and mango chutney then press down to make the sandwich.

Sunshine soup

S cowl no more with this sunny soup. Its brick yellow colour will cheer up even the greyest of days and it's a light but sustaining lunch during the warmer months, too. The quinoa and sweetcorn make this a pretty hearty meal but it's also nice with some bread and houmous on the side – or a colourful side salad.

35 minutes | Serves 4

Ingredients

– 150g quinoa, rinsed and drained
– 2 medium onions, peeled and diced
– 1 large carrot, peeled and diced
– 1-2 celery stalks, ends removed and diced
– 2 garlic cloves, peeled and finely chopped
– 200g frozen sweetcorn
– 1 tsp mustard seeds or powder
– 1 tsp coriander seeds or powder
– 2 tsp cumin seeds or powder
– 1 tsp smoked paprika
– ½ tsp chilli powder
– 2 tsp turmeric powder
– 1 tbsp coconut or olive oil
– 1 litre vegetable stock
– 1 x 400g can coconut milk
– The juice of 1 lime
– Salt and pepper

Heat the oil over a medium heat in a large pan. Add the onions and spices (if using seeds, you may want to crush or grind them slightly) and fry for 5 minutes. Add the carrots, celery, garlic and quinoa, and stir, making sure that everything is coated in the spice mixture. Season with salt and pepper and after 2 minutes, add the stock, then increase the heat and bring to the boil. Reduce the heat, cover with a lid and simmer for 15 minutes.

Now, turn up the heat and add the sweetcorn. Pour in the coconut milk, squeeze in the lime juice, stir and cook uncovered for another five minutes. If you don't want to use the coconut milk, just add more stock.

'Tuna mayo' and sweetcorn sandwich

I've always been partial to a bit of tuna mayonnaise with its perfect combination of sweet, creamy and crunchy. It's a sandwich staple and perfect in pasta salad or on a baked potato. This vegan version is just as tasty – and without the whiff of tuna – and the vinegar and mustard add a nice bit of tang. If you don't have vegan mayonnaise, use a tablespoon of tahini instead.

5-10 minutes | Makes enough for 2-3 sandwiches

Ingredients

- 1 x 400g can chickpeas, rinsed and drained
- 150g sweetcorn (fresh, canned or frozen)
- 1-2 tbsp malt or white wine vinegar
- 2 tsp wholegrain or Dijon mustard (optional)
- 2 tbsp vegan mayonnaise
- Salt and pepper

If using fresh or frozen sweetcorn, boil or steam for 4-5 minutes, then drain and set aside to cool. In a bowl, mash the chickpeas using a potato masher, then add the sweetcorn and other ingredients and mix well. Season with salt and pepper then serve in sandwiches with crisp iceberg lettuce and thinly sliced cucumber.

Roasted cauliflower
and cashew salad

The humble cauliflower's in fashion at the moment, probably because it's so versatile and is great roasted, mashed or puréed into sauces. This sumptuous salad combines crunchy cashews with a silky cauliflower dip and is full of fresh flavours. If you'd rather have sandwiches for lunch, simply blend all of the cauliflower and cashews and spread onto rye or wholemeal bread.

30-35 minutes | Serves 2

Ingredients

– 1 cauliflower, broken into florets
– 70g cashew nuts
– ½ a cucumber, diced
– ½ a 300g jar pitted black olives
– 4 big handfuls of spinach or other salad leaves
– 2 tbsp tahini
– 3 tbsp olive oil
– The juice of 1 lemon
– 2 tsp ground cumin
– 1 tsp coriander seeds (or use ground)
– 1-2 tbsp water
– A handful of sesame seeds
– Salt and pepper

Preheat the oven to 200C. In a large bowl, mix 2 tbsp olive oil, salt and pepper, 1 tsp cumin and lemon juice. Stir the cauliflower florets, making sure to coat each one in the mixture. Put them in a large ovenproof dish and place on the top shelf of the oven and roast for 15 minutes, then remove from the oven, add the cashews and roast for another 10 minutes. Remove from the oven and allow to cool slightly.

Now, put half the lemon juice, the coriander seeds, cinnamon, the rest of the olive oil and cumin, tahini and water in a food processor and blend. Take about two thirds of the roasted cauliflower and cashews and add the mixture, then blend again until fairly smooth. Add more water if needed.

In a bowl (use the same one as you used for the cauliflower), massage the spinach with the rest of the lemon juice and season with salt and pepper. Now add the remaining cauliflower and cashews, plus the cucumber and olives, and top with the dip and a smattering of pumpkin seeds. Divide into two bowls or lunch boxes.

Asian greens salad

Get all the greens in at lunchtime with this fresh and filling salad. I love edamame beans and always order them if I'm treating myself to a Wagamama. The frozen ones are really handy to keep in the freezer but if you can't get hold of them, just use some tinned chickpeas or double the amount of peas. The dressing is sweet and sharp in equal measures and you will hopefully feel a bit zestier after eating it.

20-25 minutes | Serves 2

Ingredients

– 120g frozen edamame beans
– 120g frozen peas
– 1 ripe avocado, sliced
– 100g brown or white rice
– ½ a cucumber, diced
– 2-3 large handfuls of spinach

For the dressing

– 2 tsp sesame oil
– 2 tsp soy sauce
– ½ a small red chilli
– The juice of 1 lime
– ½ tsp sesame seeds
– A handful of coriander, chopped (optional)

Cook the rice for 20 minutes or according to packet instructions. In the last 5 minutes, add the edamame beans and peas. Drain and leave to cool then place in a bowl with the spinach, avocado and cucumber. Make the dressing by mixing all the ingredients together in a bowl or glass then pour over the salad, along with the chopped coriander, if you're using it. If you're eating this away from home or have made it in advance, keep the dressing in a separate pot and pour over just before eating.

Orzo with courgettes and peas and a lemon and parsley dressing

The flavours in this salad verge on the sublime, thanks to a silky lemon and parsley dressing. Orzo's a funny little thing: it looks like rice but is actually a type of pasta but much lighter, meaning that you won't end up with the post-lunch slump. You can buy orzo in most large supermarkets but if you can't find it, quinoa, couscous or brown rice will work just as well – just adjust your cooking times.

10-15 minutes | Serves 2-3

Ingredients

For the salad

– 100g orzo pasta
– 200g peas, fresh or frozen
– 1 large courgette, diced
– 1 x 400g can chickpeas, rinsed and drained
– 2-3 handfuls of spinach
– The juice of 1 lemon
– 1 tbsp olive oil
– Salt and pepper

For the dressing

– The juice and zest of 1 unwaxed lemon (if waxed, use the juice only)
– ½ tsp mustard seeds (black or yellow) or 1 tsp wholegrain mustard
– 1 garlic clove, peeled and finely chopped
– 2 tbsp extra virgin olive oil
– 1 handful of parsley, finely chopped
– 1 tsp maple syrup
– Salt and pepper

Place the orzo into a pan of salted boiling water and cook for 6-7 minutes, then drain and set aside. Meanwhile, heat the oil in a large pan, then add the courgette and squeeze over the lemon juice. Cook for 5-6 minutes, then add the peas (shell them first if you're using fresh), chickpeas and spinach and cook for another 2-3 minutes. Stir through the orzo then quickly make the dressing. If using mustard seeds, grind them using a pestle mortar or the base of a large mug, then mix together with the other ingredients – you can do this in a bowl by with a whisk or a fork or you can pop everything into a jar and give it a good shake. Stir the dressing into the salad and serve.

Black bean, sweetcorn and coconut stew

This satisfying stew is just the tonic after a long day at the office. Black beans are full of zinc and antioxidants and the protein and fibre will keep you full, so you'll be less likely to raid the fridge later in the evening. The spiciness is tempered by the coconut cream and my special secret ingredient, banana. This is very much a case of sugar and spice and all things nice.

30 minutes | Serves 2-3

Ingredients

– 1 onion, peeled and diced
– ½ a red chilli
– 1 x 400g can black beans, rinsed and drained
– 150g sweetcorn, fresh, frozen or canned
– 1 x 400g can tomatoes, chopped or plum
– 2 tsp tomato purée
– Half a bag of spinach
– 1 banana, mashed
– 1 tsp coriander seeds, crushed (or dried coriander)
– ½ tsp chilli flakes
– 1 tbsp coconut oil
– 1 x 50g sachet coconut cream (or 200ml coconut milk)
– Flat leaf parsley
– The juice of 1 lime
– 200g brown rice

Put the brown rice on to boil and cook for 20-25 minutes, then drain. Meanwhile, on a high heat, melt the coconut oil in a large pan. Add the onions and sweat for two minutes then add the coriander and chilli flakes and cook for another two minutes. Add the tomatoes, the tomato purée, the chilli and the banana and reduce the heat. After 2 minutes, add the black beans and sweetcorn and stir well. Simmer for 5 minutes then add the coconut cream and stir through the spinach. Simmer for another 5 minutes then serve with the rice and some avocado, if you like. Scatter over some parsley and a squeeze of lime juice.

Eat your greens salad

This is a great way to use whatever green vegetables are in season. I've always thought it quite normal to put fruit in salads. I think that comes from going on day trips to Bath as a girl and eating at the Riverside Café (which is sadly no more) and being pleasantly surprised to find strawberries and grapes in my salad. The pink grapefruit adds a splash of colour and some sweet sharpness which sets off the creamy dressing.

10 minutes | Serves 2

Ingredients

– 1 x 400g can green or brown lentils, rinsed and drained
– 1 bag of spinach (or salad leaves of your choice)
– 2 large handfuls of green beans
– 2 large handfuls of tenderstem broccoli
– 2 large handfuls of asparagus
– 1 pink grapefruit, peeled and sliced lengthways
– Salt and pepper

For the dressing

– 1 tbsp tahini
– 1 tbsp olive oil
– 2 tbp water
– Salt and pepper
– The juice of half a lemon

Steam or boil the green vegetables (apart from the spinach) for 5-6 minutes, then drain and set aside to cool.

In a large bowl, season the lentils with salt and pepper and add the spinach and the cooked green vegetables. Add the pink grapefruit, then make the dressing by combining all the ingredients in a glass or jar and stirring thoroughly. Divide the salad onto two plates and drizzle over the dressing.

The simplest of stir fries

To call this cooking might be a bit of a stretch but it's quicker (and a hell of a lot cheaper) than ordering a takeaway and it's better for you, too. I make this on nights when I get home and want to spread out on the sofa as soon as possible. This is pretty effortless and you can use whatever vegetables you like. I'm a big advocate of microwave rice (which can be cooked on the hob, too) but you can always boil the regular kind if you'd prefer.

10 minutes | Serves 2

Ingredients

– 1 red pepper, sliced into thin strips
– 100g frozen peas
– 100g frozen sweetcorn
– 3-4 handfuls of spinach, fresh or frozen
– 1 pouch of microwave rice or ready-to-wok noodles
– 2-3 handfuls of cashew nuts
– 2 tbsp sesame oil
– 2-3 tbsp soy sauce
– The juice of 1 lime
– 1 red chilli (optional), finely sliced

Heat your wok until it's really hot. Add 1 tbsp oil – it should start to smoke – then add the sliced pepper, peas and sweetcorn. Stir fry for 2-3 minutes, then add the rice or noodles and use a wooden spoon to break them up. Add the spinach, and after 2 minutes add the cashew nuts, cook for another minute then remove from the heat. In a bowl or jar, quickly whisk together the rest of the oil, the soy sauce, lime juice and chilli. Divide the stir fry between two plates or bowls and pour over the dressing.

Speedy spaghetti with olive and tomato pesto

For me, a bowl of spaghetti is somehow both soothing and sophisticated. This can be made in under ten minutes and I recommend that you always serve generous portions. For this dish, you can use fresh or tinned tomatoes. I sometimes use wholemeal spelt spaghetti because it feels a bit healthier but any version will do. If you're really hungry and want a heartier meal, add a tin of lentils or chickpeas or some crushed nuts.

20 minutes | Serves 2

Ingredients

– 150g spaghetti
– 1 punnet of cherry or plum tomatoes, halved (or 1 x 400g can chopped tomatoes)
– 1 330g jar pitted black olives, drained (keep some of the brine for the pesto)
– 2 tsp pine nuts
– The juice of 1 lemon
– A handful of basil leaves, torn, plus extra for garnishing
– 2 tbsp extra virgin olive oil
– Salt and pepper

Boil a pan of salted water and cook the spaghetti for 8–10 minutes, then drain. Meanwhile, make your pesto: place half the tomatoes and olives (and a teaspoon of its brine) in a food processor with the pine nuts, olive oil, basil leaves, plus half the lemon juice. Blend until you have a coarse paste.

Put the drained spaghetti back in the pan and stir through the pesto. Add the remainder of the tomatoes and olives and stir through, then warm over a medium heat. Serve in bowls with extra basil and pine nuts and squeeze over the rest of the lemon juice.

Cumin-roasted carrots with hazelnuts and brown rice

This reminds me of the hearty salad bowls I sometimes enjoy at Crumbs, a plant-eater's paradise with cafes in Cardiff and Swansea. It has a wonderfully wholesome texture to it, thanks to the hazelnuts, roasted carrots and chewy brown rice, and the cumin and maple syrup glaze is heavenly. This is one to eat when you need a vitamin hit.

30–35 minutes | Serves 2

Ingredients

– 2-3 large carrots, sliced in half, lengthways
– 200g brown rice, rinsed and drained
– ½ a head of broccoli, broken into florets
– ½ a cucumber, diced
– 50g hazelnuts, cut in half
– ½ a 330g jar pitted black olives
– 2 big handfuls of spinach or other salad leaves
– Flat-leaf parsley (optional), roughly chopped

For the glaze

– 3 tbsp olive oil
– 2 tbsp maple syrup
– 1½ tsp cumin powder
– ½ tsp cinnamon powder
– 1 tbsp water
– Salt and pepper

Preheat the oven to 200C. Bring a pan of salted water to the boil and parboil the carrots for 5 minutes. Drain and set aside.

Make the glaze by whisking together all the ingredients in a bowl. Use half of the glaze to coat the base of an ovenproof dish, then add the carrots, making sure that both sides are coated. Place in the oven and cook for 15 minutes, then add the broccoli and hazelnuts plus a drizzle of oil and cook for another 10-15 minutes.

Meanwhile, bring a large pan of water to the boil and cook the rice for 20-25 minutes. Drain and set aside. In a large bowl, add the cooked rice, spinach, cucumber, black olives and parsley and pour over the rest of the cumin glaze. Divide onto two plates or dishes then add the carrots, broccoli and hazelnuts and serve, perhaps with a squeeze of lemon juice.

Sweet potato, chickpea and olive stew with harissa

This is a seriously good stew and so easy to make. It's just as good in the winter as it is in the summer and very nice with a glass of wine. It's the harissa with all its sweet spiciness that really makes this so tasty. You can find it at most larger supermarkets or international stores but if you can't track it down, try using a teaspoon each of smoked and sweet paprika.

40-45 minutes | Serves 4

Ingredients

- 1 large sweet potato, scrubbed or peeled and diced
- 1 small onion, peeled and diced
- 1 x 400g can chickpeas, rinsed and drained
- 1 x 400g can tomatoes, chopped or plum
- The juice of 1 lemon
- 2 garlic cloves, peeled and chopped or crushed
- ½ a 330g jar pitted black olives
- 3 tsps harissa paste
- 2 tsp tomato purée
- 1 tbsp olive oil
- Salt and pepper
- Chopped flat-leaf parsley (optional)

Place a large pan over a medium heat then add the oil and the sweet potato. Cook for 5 minutes, then add the onion and garlic and cook for another 5 minutes, stirring frequently.

Add the tomatoes, then fill the empty can with water and add to the pan. Season with salt and pepper then turn up the heat and cook for 10 minutes before adding the chickpeas, olives, harissa paste, tomato purée and lemon juice.

Reduce the heat, place a lid on the pan and cook for a further 15-20 minutes, adding more water if you think it's necessary. Scatter over the parsley, if you like, and serve with green vegetables or salad.

Baked lemony 'feta' with lentils

I've never been one for vegan cheese but things have changed a lot in the couple of years since I turned vegan. Now you can buy all kinds of dairy-free cheese from the supermarket and most of them are pretty tasty. I especially like the Greek style (or 'feta') version as it's just as creamy and slightly tangy as the real deal. This hearty dish takes next to no time to make and is all lovely and lemony. If you want to save a bit of time, you can use tinned lentils instead; just gently warm them in a pan.

30 minutes | Serves 2

Ingredients

– 200g vegan feta cheese
– 150g green or brown lentils, rinsed and drained
– 10-12 cherry tomatoes
– ½ a 300g jar pitted black olives
– 80g spinach
– The juice of 2 lemons
– 2 tbsp olive oil
– A few sprigs of thyme (or ½ tsp dried)
– A handful of flat-leaf parsley

Preheat the oven to 180°C. Put the lentils into a saucepan with cold water. Bring to the boil and cook on a high heat for 10 minutes then reduce the heat and simmer for 15–20 minutes or until tender.

While the lentils are cooking, crumble the feta into large chunks and place into a large ovenproof dish. Add the tomatoes and olives, then make your dressing. Mix the juice of one lemon juice and 1 tbsp olive oil with the thyme and pour over the contents of the dish. Bake in the oven for 5–10 minutes, depending on how firm or melted you like your cheese.

When the lentils are cooked, drain and return to the pan then add the rest of the lemon juice and olive oil and place on a low heat. Add the spinach and warm for 5 minutes or until it has wilted. Serve with the feta, tomatoes and olives and scatter over the parsley.

Quick chickpea and cauliflower curry

This quick curry is perfect for when you've had a long day at work and need something nourishing. If you want to turn it into a treat, it goes well with a couple of beers and some poppadoms with mango chutney and lime pickle. Chickpeas are full of fibre and protein and they're cheap and filling, too. For this recipe, I use curry paste from a jar (just check the label to make sure it's vegan), although you can grind up spices like coriander and cumin seeds and make your own if you prefer (see the recipe on page 31). If you're feeling indulgent, chuck in a can of coconut milk for extra richness.

35-40 minutes | Serves 4

Ingredients

– 1 x 400g can chickpeas, rinsed and drained
– 1 medium cauliflower, broken into small florets
– 1 punnet of cherry tomatoes, chopped in half (or 1 x 400g can tomatoes, chopped or plum)
– 1 tsp fresh ginger root, peeled and grated
– 1 garlic clove, peeled and crushed, grated or finely chopped
– 1 red onion, peeled and finely chopped
– 3 tbsp curry paste
– 100g of spinach (fresh or frozen)
– 1 tbp olive or coconut oil
– 300g brown rice, rinsed and drained

Bring a large pan of water to the boil and cook the rice for 20-25 minutes. Meanwhile, heat the oil in a large pan over a medium heat. Add the cauliflower florets and onions and fry for 5 minutes until soft. Add the ginger, garlic and curry paste, and stir. Add a little water if it begins to stick. After a minute, add the tomatoes to the pan and squash them gently with a wooden spoon.

Keep stirring the mixture regularly and gradually add a mugful or so of water. Turn up the heat and after about 10 minutes, add the chickpeas and another half a mug of water. Give it a good stir and add the spinach and cover with a lid. Cook for another 15-20 minutes then serve with the rice and some poppadoms, if you like.

Pearl barley risotto with mushrooms and thyme

It's the veggie option on menus up and down the country, but risotto doesn't have to be boring. This version uses pearl barley which is rich in fibre and is much cheaper to buy than risotto rice. It also has a nuttier texture and taste. This doesn't take long to cook and the occasional stirring can be quite meditative, especially after a taxing day.

30 minutes | Serves 4

Ingredients

– 200g pearl barley
– 100g mushrooms, sliced
– 100ml white wine
– 500ml vegetable stock
– 2 shallots, peeled and diced
– 2 garlic cloves, peeled and finely chopped
– 1 small carrot, peeled and diced
– 1 celery stalk, ends removed and diced
– 5-6 sprigs of thyme
– The juice of 1 lemon
– 1 tbsp olive oil
– 50g pine nuts
– Black pepper

Heat the oil in a large pan, then add the shallots, carrot and celery and sauté for 3 minutes. Add the garlic and thyme and cook for a further 2 minutes. Add the pearl barley to the pan with the white wine. Mix well, coating each grain in oil – add a little extra if necessary. Add the mushrooms and cook the mixture for another 2-3 minutes. Add a ladleful of the hot stock to the pearl barley and stir well. Bring to a simmer as the liquid is absorbed by the rice. Continue adding more stock, a ladleful at a time, letting the pearl barley absorb it gradually; do this for about 15-20 minutes, until the pearl barley is soft. Add the lemon juice, black pepper and pine nuts and serve with green vegetables or on its own. Squeeze over some more lemon juice and a drizzle of extra virgin olive oil, if you like.

Beat the blues salad

This colourful plate of cheer combines beetroot and orange with salty black olives. I used to make this salad with mackerel but tofu does the trick now. You will need to press and marinate it (you can, of course, buy the pre-smoked stuff but it's not always that easy to find) which takes a little time but I promise you, it's worth it. You will need an hour or so to press and marinate the tofu so I'd suggest doing this in the morning before you head to work – or even the night before.

15 minutes, plus extra time for preparing the tofu | Serves 3-4

Ingredients

For the salad

– 1 x 400g block firm tofu
– 2 bags of lettuce or spinach
– 1 cucumber, diced
– 2-3 large beetroots, peeled and sliced (or use the vacuum-packed kind)
– 3 tsp capers, drained
– 1 330g jar pitted black olives
– 2 oranges, divided into segments
– 1 tbsp sesame oil
– Flat-leaf parsley (optional)

For the marinade

– 3 tbsp soy sauce
– 1 tsp sea salt
– 2 tbsp maple syrup
– 1 tsp smoked paprika
– ½ tsp cinnamon

Take the tofu and use kitchen roll or a clean tea towel to blot and absorb all its water. Take a heavy wooden chopping board or a hardback book and place it on top of the wrapped tofu. This will press down on it and absorb excess moisture. Leave for 30 minutes or more then slice into medium-sized strips.

Make the marinade by mixing together all the ingredients. Pour into the base of a large dish and place the slices of tofu into it, making sure to turn them so that both sides are covered in the marinade. Leave to marinate for 30 minutes.

Heat the sesame oil in a large frying pan over a medium heat. Fry the tofu slices for 5-10 minutes or until golden brown, turning occasionally – you may need to do this in two batches. Remove from the pan and set aside while you make the salad. Simply combine all the ingredients in a large bowl then drizzle with a little sesame oil. Divide into bowls and serve with the smoked tofu. Garnish with the parsley.

Baked sweet potato with a roasted aubergine and cauliflower harissa dip

There's nothing like coming home to a baked potato. Sweet potatoes count as one of your five a day (unlike regular spuds) and contain vitamin A and C and some calcium, potassium and iron, too. Roasted cauliflower is one of my favourite things to eat and, when combined with sweet and mild aubergine and spicy harissa, it verges on the extraordinary. Once you've tried this dreamy dip you'll never want to put anything else on your potatoes. This takes a little bit more than half an hour but you can leave the vegetables in the oven while you do something else.

40-45 minutes | Serves 2

Ingredients

– 2 large sweet potatoes
– 2 tbsp olive oil
– Salt and pepper

For the topping

– 1 medium aubergine, sliced
– Half a large head of cauliflower, broken into florets
– 2 tsp harissa paste
– The juice of 1 lemon
– 2 tbsp tahini
– 4 tbsp olive oil

Preheat the oven to 200C. Scrub the sweet potatoes, pat dry and prick with a fork, then rub with a little olive oil and a pinch of sea salt and black pepper and place on a baking tray in the oven. Put the cauliflower and aubergine in a large ovenproof dish, drizzle over 2 tbsp of olive oil and season with salt and pepper and put in the oven with the potatoes. Roast for 30 minutes then remove the cauliflower and aubergine from the oven and leave to cool. Roast the potatoes for another 10 minutes.

 Put the cauliflower and aubergine in a food processor with the other ingredients and blend until fairly smooth. Take the potatoes out of the oven, slice in half and dollop over the topping. Serve with green vegetables, a squeeze of lemon juice and a drizzle of extra virgin olive oil.

Cheat's Buddha bowl

When did Buddha bowls become all the rage? The appeal is obvious: a combination of protein, grains and vegetables makes for a hearty and nourishing and meal. And anything served in a bowl is instant comfort food, right? In fact, I think I read somewhere that it's so-called because the bowl is meant to replicate Buddha's rounded belly – or maybe it's to do with taking a balanced approach to eating. Either way, it's quick, easy and tasty so it gets my vote. I call this a cheat's version because it uses curry paste instead of fresh spices. If you want to take a further shortcut, use microwave rice.

20-25 minutes | Serves 2

Ingredients

– 100g frozen peas
– 100g brown rice, rinsed and drained
– 8 small mushrooms, thinly sliced
– 1 avocado, peeled and stoned
– 2 tbsp vegan Thai green curry paste
– 5-6 radishes, thinly sliced
– Half a bag of spinach
– Half a head of broccoli, cut into florets
– 1 tbsp coconut, sesame or olive oil
– 2 tbsp soy sauce
– 1 tsp sesame seeds
– The juice of 1 lime

Bring a pan of water to the boil and add the rice. Reduce the heat and cook for 15 minutes. Add the peas and cook for another 5 minutes. In a large pan, heat the oil over a medium heat and sauté the mushrooms and broccoli for 3-4 minutes, then add the spinach and soy sauce. Cook for another 2-3 minutes or until the spinach has wilted.

When the rice and peas are cooked, drain and return to the saucepan, then stir through the curry paste. Divide between two bowls and on one side of the dish, place the mushrooms, spinach and broccoli. On the other side, layer over the sliced avocado and radishes. Sprinkle over the sesame seeds and squeeze over the lime juice.

Panzanella with smashed beans

I'd eat bread and tomatoes all day every day if I could. This traditional Tuscan salad is a good way to use up stale bread and adding creamy mashed butterbeans makes it a more filling meal. It's generally eaten as a summer dish but it can be enjoyed all year round and is especially good if you need to cook a simple supper for friends.

20-25 minutes | Serves 2 hungry (greedy) people

Ingredients

– For the panzanella
– Half a ciabatta loaf (or two rolls), torn
– 3-4 vine tomatoes, quartered
– 10-12 cherry or plum tomatoes, halved
– 3 tbsp capers
– 2 handfuls fresh basil

For the dressing

– 3 tbsp olive oil
– 1 ½ white wine vinegar (or use balsamic)
– 1 garlic clove, peeled and crushed

For the beans

– 1 x 400g x can butterbeans, rinsed and drained
– 1 tsbp olive oil
– 1 garlic clove, peeled and crushed
– 3-4 handfuls spinach
– The juice of 1 lemon
– Salt and pepper

Preheat the oven to 130C. Put the ciabatta pieces on a baking tray in the oven for 10 minutes to dry out. Allow to cool. Meanwhile, make the dressing by whisking the olive oil with the white wine vinegar and garlic. Season with salt and pepper, then set aside. Toss the tomatoes, capers, basil and ciabatta in a serving dish. Drizzle over the dressing then toss again until evenly coated. Leave to stand for 15 minutes to allow the flavours to infuse.

Meanwhile, make the beans. In a pan, heat the oil over a medium heat and add the beans, garlic and spinach. Heat for 2-3 minutes, stirring continuously, until the spinach has wilted. Transfer the mixture to a bowl and leave to cool for two minutes. Squeeze over the lemon juice, season with salt and pepper and stir well. Mash roughly with a fork or potato masher. Serve with the panzanella salad.

Easy peas-y soup

A bowl of soup (like a cup of tea) can fix most things and is perfect for getting your five-a-day in one meal. Making it is also very therapeutic (I like to stick on a Woman's Hour podcast while I'm chopping) and a great way to use up whatever vegetables are in the fridge. This is a really simple soup to make and can be enjoyed all year round – just use whatever's in season.

25-30 minutes | Serves 4

Ingredients

- 1 tbsp olive oil
- 1 onion, diced
- ½ a red chilli, finely chopped
- 2 garlic cloves, peeled and finely chopped
- 300g baby new potatoes, scrubbed
- 300g Savoy cabbage, roughly chopped
- 300g peas, fresh or frozen
- 1 litre vegetable stock
- A few leaves of fresh basil
- A few leaves of fresh mint
- Salt and pepper

Heat the oil in a large pot over a medium to high heat. Add the onion, potatoes, garlic and chilli and fry for 5 minutes, stirring occasionally. Add the hot stock, bring to the boil, then reduce the heat, cover the pan with a lid and simmer for 10-15 minutes or until the potatoes are tender. Add the cabbage and cook for a couple of minutes, then add the peas, basil and mint. Cook for another 5 minutes, then season with salt and pepper and serve with crusty bread or on its own.

Chocolate mousse

If you fancy a sweet treat or if you're cooking for friends and need a quick dessert, you can make this quickly and leave it to set in the fridge while you're eating dinner. The surprise ingredient here is chickpea water, also known as aquafaba. It might sound crazy but it acts in the same way as egg whites and gives you a light and fluffy mousse. You really should give this a try because it's truly delicious. I find that cheap supermarket dark or plain chocolate works well here as it's usually higher in sugar.

20-25 minutes, plus chilling time | Serves 2

Ingredients

– 150g dark chocolate
– A dash of plant milk
– 120ml chickpea water
– 1 tsp vanilla extract
– A pinch of sea salt (optional)

Carefully place a heatproof bowl over a pan of boiling water and add the chocolate and plant milk and stir gently until melted. Remove the bowl from the pan and set aside to cool slightly. If you have a microwave, heat the bowl on a medium power at 60-second intervals until melted.

Pour the chickpea water (one can should give you about 120ml water and you save the chickpeas for cooking something else) into a large bowl and whisk vigorously for 15 minutes, or until you have stiff peaks. This requires a strong wrist although you can use an electric whisk if you have one. To check if you have said stiff peaks, tilt the bowl slightly – if the water runs down the edge, you need to whisk more. When stiff, fold in the chocolate mixture then add the vanilla extract and the salt and stir well.

Pour into glasses or ramekins and leave in the fridge to set for at least an hour.

Something for the weekend

Ah, the weekend. A chance to switch off and take things a little bit more slowly. For me, it's also the opportunity to take a bit more time when cooking and eating. What's better than a long lie-in followed by a lazy breakfast? The real beauty of downing tools for 48 hours is that you can eat whatever you like whenever you like. This collection includes a few Friday night 'fake aways', leisurely brunches, relaxed meals to impress family, friends or just yourself, and some traditional Sunday favourites with a twist.

To-fish and chips with minty mushy peas

When I was a kid, we'd often have fish and chips on a Friday evening and I loved to douse everything with vinegar and tomato ketchup – something I still do. This vegan version of the takeaway staple is getting more and more popular at restaurants across the UK and it's pretty easy to make yourself. Once you've marinated the tofu and made the batter, it's simply a case of deep frying which can be a little messy but it's worth it. This isn't the healthiest of meals but the chips are oven-baked plus the mushy peas give you a one of your five-a-day – and anyway, it's the weekend!

1 hour 30 minutes, plus extra time for preparing the tofu | Serves 2

Ingredients

For the to-fish

– 1 400g block firm tofu
– The juice of 1 lemon
– 1 tbsp olive oil
– 1 tbsp white wine vinegar
– 1 tbsp soy sauce
– Salt and pepper
– 200ml vegetable oil (or more, depending on the size of your pan)

For the batter

– 100ml fizzy water
– 100ml plant milk
– 120g self-raising flour
– Salt and pepper

For the chips

– 2-3 large floury potatoes (Maris Piper or King Edward are good)
– 1 tbsp olive oil
– Salt and pepper

For the mushy peas

– 100g frozen peas
– 2-3 fresh mint leaves, chopped finely
– The juice of half a lemon
– 1 tsp soy sauce
– Lemon wedges, to serve

Take the tofu and use kitchen roll or a clean tea towel to blot and absorb all its water. Take two heavy wooden chopping boards and place on either side of the block to 'press' it and absorb excess moisture. If you can, put something heavy, like a hardback book, on top of the chopping board to weigh it down further. Leave for at least 30 minutes then slice into medium-sized strips. Now make your marinade by mixing together the olive oil, vinegar, soy sauce and lemon juice. Pour into a large dish, then coat both sides of the tofu strips with the mixture and leave to marinate for 30 minutes.

While the tofu is marinating, start making the chips. Preheat the oven to 200C. Peel the potatoes and cut them into long, thick chip shapes, then rinse under the cold tap and pat dry with a tea towel.

Spread the chips on a large non-stick baking tray and toss with the oil and salt and pepper. Lie them flat in a single layer and roast for 45-50 mins, turning now and then. When cooked, they should be golden brown and crisp with a light, fluffy centre.

Meanwhile, make your batter. In a large bowl, whisk together all the ingredients and set aside. Now take a large pan and pour in the vegetable oil. You'll need enough to fill half the pan so that when you fry the tofu it's fully submerged in the oil.

Heat the oil on a high heat (use the back ring on the hob and be careful that it doesn't splatter) and add a tiny bit of batter mix to check that it's hot enough. If you get batter, you're good to go. Take a strip of tofu from the dish and dip into the batter, making sure that both sides are coated. Using tongs, drop the tofu into the hot oil and fry for 3-4 minutes or until golden brown – you'll need to turn it every so often. Remove from the pan and place on some kitchen roll to absorb some of the oil. Do this with all the tofu pieces – you can cook a few in the pan at the same time. If you want your tofu to be extra crispy, dip it in the batter mix again after frying then cook them again in the hot oil. You may need to top up the oil in the pan and make more batter mixture if you decide to do this.

Check on your chips (they should be almost ready) and boil a small pan of water for the peas. Boil the peas for 3-4 minutes, then rinse in cold water and drain. Set aside to cool slightly while you get the chips out of the oven. Now, add the mint, lemon juice and soy sauce and roughly mash with a fork or potato masher. Serve with the to-fish and chips, with some lemon wedges to squeeze over, and enjoy!

Caponata

This sweet and slightly sour Sicilian stew is simply the best. I like to use tinned or sundried tomatoes for a richer flavour but you can use fresh when they're in season. It's sometimes served as an appetiser but with pasta, rice or crusty bread, it makes a filling meal. The chilli's optional and you can use rosemary or another herb instead of the thyme, if you like.

1 hour 20 minutes | Serves 4

Ingredients

– 4 tbsp olive oil
– 2 large aubergines, cut into 2cm cubes
– 3 stalks celery, ends removed and diced
– 3 shallots, peeled and diced
– 2 garlic cloves, peeled finely chopped
– ½ chilli, finely chopped
– A few sprigs of thyme
– 1 x 400g can tomatoes, chopped or plum
– 2 tbsp tomato purée
– 2 tsp capers
– 50ml red wine or balsamic vinegar
– A handful of toasted pine nuts or flaked almonds to garnish (optional)
– A few basil leaves to garnish

Pour 1 tbsp olive oil into a large saucepan or casserole, place over a medium heat and add the aubergines. Cook for a good 20-25 mins until they are soft. Scoop the aubergines out of the pan and set aside. Add the rest of the oil plus the shallots, celery, garlic, chilli and thyme, and cook for about 5 minutes until they are soft and translucent. Add the tomatoes and cook slowly, so they break down and turn to a soft mush, then add the aubergines back to the pan. Now put in the tomato purée, capers and vinegar, season well and cover with a lid. Cook over a low heat for 20-25 minutes, until all the vegetables are soft. Stir gently so it doesn't break up too much. Serve the warm caponata scattered with flaked almonds or pine nuts if using.

Lemon tofu and fried rice

As a child, Chinese food was a big treat and every once in a while, Mum would come home with a bagful of oven meals from Marks and Spencer. It was only when I got older that I tried the takeaway kind, but for me, it was way too greasy.

I loved umami flavours from a young age so sweet and sour sauce was a firm favourite, but what I remember the most is lemon chicken. This is a vegan version of that with fried rice. When life gives you lemons, make this.

50-55 minutes, plus time for preparing the tofu | Serves 2

Ingredients

For the lemon tofu

– 1 x 400g block firm tofu
– 1 yellow pepper, cut into thin strips
– The juice of 4 lemons
– 1 tbsp flour
– 1 tbsp soy sauce
– 4 tsps sugar
– 1 tbsp sesame oil

For the fried rice

– 125g brown rice
– 100g peas, fresh or frozen
– 1 tbsp sesame oil

Take the tofu and use kitchen roll or a clean tea towel to blot and absorb all its water. Take a heavy wooden chopping board or a hardback book and place it on top of the wrapped tofu. This will press down on it and absorb excess moisture. Leave for 30 minutes then slice into medium-sized strips.

Preheat the oven to 200C and in an oven-proof dish, mix the soy sauce, flour and juice from two of the lemons. Coat both sides of the tofu strips with the mixture and leave to marinate for 15 minutes then bake for 25-30 minutes, turning every so often.

Meanwhile, rinse and drain the rice and add to a pan of cold water. Bring to the boil and cook for 20 minutes then drain. In a large pan or wok, heat the sesame oil and add the rice and peas and fry for ten minutes.

Remove the tofu from the oven. Mix together the remainder of the lemon juice, the sugar and the sesame oil and heat in a large pan. Add the sliced pepper and fry for a minute or two before adding the tofu. Cook for another 5-6 minutes until the tofu is glazed in the sauce, then serve with the fried rice.

Cheering chilli with guacamole

This one's sure to warm the cockles and not just because it's hot. It's my 'go to' dish when friends are coming over for dinner because it's such a crowd pleaser and it goes well with lots of red wine – or tequila if you're feeling wild. It's easy to make and once everything's chopped and in the pan, it can be left on the hob for as long as you like to let the flavours mellow. I like to serve it with some zesty guacamole and vegan yogurt to temper the heat. The spice ratio here is merely a guide so use more chilli and spices if you want more heat – just keep tasting as you go along. Oh, and you can use whatever canned beans you have in the cupboard; I've just used my favourites here.

1 hour | Serves 4-5

Ingredients

For the chilli

– 1 tbsp olive oil
– 1 red pepper, cut into chunks
– 1 green pepper, cut into chunks
– 2 onions, peeled and diced
– 2 garlic cloves, peeled and finely chopped
– 1 red chilli, finely chopped and deseeded – unless you want extra spice
– 1 tsp chilli powder
– 1 tsp smoked paprika
– 1 tsp ground cumin
– 2 tsp cinnamon
– 2 x 400g cans tomatoes, chopped or plum
– 3 tsp tomato purée
– 1 x 400g can black beans, rinsed and drained
– 1 x 400g can kidney beans, rinsed and drained
– 1 x 400g can black-eyed beans, rinsed and drained
– 2 squares of dark chocolate
– Salt and pepper
– 300g brown rice, rinsed and drained

For the guacamole

– 2 large, ripe avocados
– ½ a red chilli, finely chopped
– The juice of 1 lime

Put the rice in a saucepan of salted water, bring to the boil and cook for 20-25 minutes. Meanwhile, heat the oil over a medium to low heat, then add the onions and fry for 5 minutes. Add the garlic, chilli and peppers, plus some salt and pepper, and cook for another 2 minutes. Now add the tinned tomatoes (half fill one of the empty cans with water and add this to the pan, too), tomato purée, spices and chocolate, stir well and season with salt and pepper. Bring to the boil then reduce the heat, place a lid on the pan and simmer for 30-40 minutes (this really lets the flavours take shape but if you're short of time, 20 minutes will do), stirring occasionally. Add the beans and cook for another 10 minutes.

Serve with the drained brown rice, the guacamole and the chopped coriander and red onion, if using. To make the guacamole, cut the avocados in half, remove the stones and, using a fork, mash together with the chilli. Squeeze over the lime juice and stir through. If you have any leftover chilli (it's unlikely though), you can freeze it – or serve alongside the tacos with pulled jackfruit on page 128.

Chocolate chip cookies

These are more biscuity than chewy, and remind me of the Maryland cookies I ate by the dozen as a kid. The recipe is really easy to follow but be careful: the cookie dough is seriously tasty and it will be hard not to eat it all before it makes it into the oven.

45 minutes | Makes around 12-16 cookies

Ingredients

– 225g plain flour
– 1 tsp baking powder
– 225g vegan margarine, at room temperature
– 100g caster sugar
– 100g dark or dairy-free chocolate chips

Preheat the oven to 150C. In a large bowl, cream the margarine and sugar together until light and fluffy. Gradually sieve through the flour and baking powder and mix well. Then stir through the chocolate chips.

Roll or scoop the dough into small balls and place onto a large ungreased baking tray (you may need to use more than one), making sure that they're about 3cm apart. Bake for 25-30 minutes or until the cookies are a light golden-brown colour. Remove from the tray(s) and leave them to cool.

One pan brunch

My friends used to joke that I was obsessed with 'doing brunch' and even in a pre-Instagram age it was all the rage thanks to Sex and the City. Years of watching Carrie Bradshaw and co catching up over Eggs Benedict in fashionable Manhattan eateries certainly glamorised the most important meal of the day and now we're just as likely to enjoy brunch (and take countless photos of it) at home as we are at a restaurant or café. My favourite way to make brunch at home is to throw a few things in a pan and then eat it with a pot of coffee and the papers. This one pan version is really easy to make, although if you want to make it extra special, serve with the scrambled tofu (page 103) or some muhammara (page 107)

20-25 minutes | Serves 2

Ingredients

– 14-15 small potatoes, diced into small pieces
– 4-5 large vine tomatoes, whole
– 10 mushrooms, sliced
– 100g spinach
– The juice of 1 lemon
– 1 tbsp olive oil
– 3-4 sprigs of thyme
– Salt and pepper

Heat the oil in a pan on a medium heat. Add the potatoes, thyme and a squeeze of lemon and season with salt and pepper. Cook for 10 minutes, stirring every so often. Add the mushrooms and tomatoes and another squeeze of lemon and cook for another 5 minutes then add the spinach and more lemon juice. Cook for another 2-3 minutes, or until the spinach has wilted, then serve. Add extra lemon juice and Tabasco sauce, if you like.

Scrambled tofu

Breakfast has always been my favourite meal of the day. When I was growing up, it was a rushed affair and during the school week, we'd hurriedly scoff cereal or a bit of toast before running to catch the school bus in time.

Come the weekend, we'd get up late (we're a family of night owls) and Mum would make us scrambled eggs. A dollop of creamy, golden goodness piled onto hot, buttered toast was the perfect start to my Saturday. Now I look for vegan alternatives to get my 'egg' fix and I find that tofu works a treat. Add as much or as little spice to this as you like – and if you prefer, use dried sage or thyme instead, but do use the turmeric if you can as it gives the tofu a gloriously sunny colour.

10-15 minutes, plus extra for preparing the tofu | Serves 2

Ingredients

– 1 x 400g block firm tofu
– 1 garlic clove, peeled and finely chopped
– The juice of 1 lemon
– 1 tsp ground cumin
– 1 tsp ground turmeric
– Pinch of chilli flakes or powder
– A little plant milk (optional)
– Salt and pepper

Take the tofu and use kitchen roll or a clean tea towel to blot and absorb all its water. Take two heavy wooden chopping boards and place on either side of the block to 'press' it and absorb excess moisture. If you can, put something heavy, like a hardback book, on top of the chopping board to weigh it down further. Leave for 15-20 minutes then put in a bowl and mash it up with a fork. Add the garlic, lemon juice, salt, cumin, turmeric and chilli and mash together. Heat the oil in a non-stick pan over a low heat and cook the tofu for 5 minutes, stirring regularly. Stir through a little plant milk if you want a creamier consistency. Once it's brown, it's ready. Serve with toast, avocado, tomatoes – or whatever you like.

Banana and peanut butter loaf

I live by the motto that brown bananas should never be binned. We often end up with a few overripe 'uns in the fruit bowl which invariably get turned into banana bread. In this recipe, I've added peanut butter for a richer texture – and a bit of protein. You can eat it for breakfast, dessert or as a snack (it's extra tasty spread with vegan margarine or served with dairy-free yogurt or ice cream) and it'll keep for 2-3 days in an airtight container.

50 minutes | Makes 1 medium-sized loaf

Ingredients

– 225g plain flour
– 2tsp baking powder
– 5 very ripe bananas
– 50ml vegetable, olive, sunflower or coconut oil (plus a little bit extra for greasing the loaf tin)
– 100ml plant milk
– 2-3 tsp peanut butter
– 100g brown sugar
– 2 tbsp maple syrup
– 2 tsp cinnamon

For the topping (optional)

– 1 tablespoon maple syrup
– 2 bananas
– 2 tsp cinnamon

Preheat the oven to 200C. In a large bowl, mash the bananas with a fork, then add the oil and sugar and mix with a wooden spoon. Sieve over the flour and baking powder and mix together. Add the other ingredients and stir thoroughly. Grease a 9×5 inch loaf pan, add the cake mixture and place on the middle shelf of the oven. Bake for 35-40 minutes or until golden brown. Allow to cool, then serve in slices, perhaps with some vegan margarine or ice cream.

If you want to add the topping, heat a medium saucepan over medium heat and add the maple syrup. Slice bananas into thin discs, place in the pan and sprinkle with the cinnamon. Cook for a minute, then flip the banana slices over and cook for another minute until golden brown. Allow to cool slightly, then spread evenly over the top of the loaf.

Muhammara

Whether you're spending a Saturday night in front of the telly or you're having some drinks at the house before you head out into town, it's good to have a few nibbles to hand. Houmous is a classic but why not try its younger, hipper sister, the magnificently moreish muhammara? The traditional recipe uses Aleppo pepper but chilli flakes (or powder) is just fine – and if you can't find pomegranate molasses, you can substitute it with maple syrup and balsamic vinegar. Lots of people remove the skins from the peppers but I don't think you really need to.

This stuff is pretty versatile: you can spoon it onto pasta, bread (obviously), baked potatoes and salads, and it's a great addition to brunch – it goes really well with tomatoes and avocado.

45-50 minutes | Makes enough for a large jar

Ingredients

– 3 red peppers, cut into half and seeds removed
– 60g walnuts
– 1 tbsp pomegranate molasses (or 1 tsp maple syrup and 2 tsps balsamic vinegar)
– 1 tbsp extra virgin olive oil
– ½ tsp chilli flakes
– 1 tsp ground cumin
– ½ tsp salt
– The juice of 1 lemon
– 1 garlic clove, peeled
– 1 tsp tomato purée

Preheat the oven to 200C and roast the peppers with a drizzle of olive oil and some salt and pepper for 35-40 minutes. Remove from the oven and leave to cool. While the peppers are cooking, take a dry pan and gently roast the walnuts for a few minutes, being careful not to let them burn. Once they're cool, blitz in a food processor until they have a coarse consistency and then add the peppers and all the other ingredients and whizz until you have a fairly smooth paste. Taste and add more oil and/or molasses if needed.

Serve with an extra drizzle of olive oil and pomegranate molasses, if you like.

Jumpin Jack Flash burgers

As a kid, Saturday mornings meant a long lie-in and hanging around in our pyjamas while Mum played the Rolling Stones over and over again. After a big brunch, we'd have an early tea, and quite often it would be a Linda McCartney veggie burger with oven chips and beans. These burgers with pulled jackfruit are an extension of that – and a tribute to my earliest rock 'n' roll influence. If you don't like dill, leave it out and use another herb instead.

1 hour 20 minutes | Serves 4

Ingredients

– 2 x 400g cans jackfruit in brine, rinsed and drained
– 1 x 400g can chickpeas, rinsed and drained
– 1 medium onion, peeled and finely diced
– 2 garlic cloves, peeled and finely diced
– 1 heaped tsp Marmite
– 5-6 mushrooms, cut into small chunks
– 5 tsp dill, finely chopped (optional)
– 2-3 tsp tomato purée
– 1 tsp smoked paprika
– 3-4 tbsp plain flour, plus extra for dusting
– Salt and pepper
– 3-4 tbsp olive oil

Rub the drained jackfruit between your fingers until it becomes stringy – the stems and seeds are edible so use these, too. In a large pan, fry the onions and garlic in 1 tbsp olive oil in a large pan for 10 minutes, or until they are browned. Add the jackfruit and paprika, the Marmite and about 75ml boiling water, then pour into the pan. Stir and simmer for 5-10 minutes, stirring occasionally. Meanwhile, in a large bowl, roughly mash the chickpeas with a potato masher or fork. When the jackfruit mixture is cooked, tip it into this bowl.

Using the same pan, heat 1 tbsp oil and fry the mushrooms for about 5 minutes, until golden brown. Add to the bowl with the tomato purée, dill and flour, plus salt and pepper, and combine. Lightly flour a kitchen surface and make four burger shaped patties, making sure to coat both sides with flour. Place on a plate and chill for at least 30 minutes.

Take the burgers from the fridge and heat 1-2 tbsp oil in a large frying pan over a medium heat. Fry for 5-10 minutes or until golden brown, turning frequently. Serve in burger baps with iceberg lettuce, sliced tomato and vegan mayonnaise.

Saturday night spaghetti bolognese

I grew up in the nineties when Italian food was still a fairly new phenomenon in the UK – or at least in south Wales – and my late grandmother, admittedly a fussy eater, refused to try pasta. Mum, thankfully, was more adventurous and sometimes, after a Saturday afternoon shopping in town, she'd stick on the stereo and make spaghetti bolognese while we watched Noel's House Party. The sauce was often made with minced beef, but sometimes we had it with lentils – and here is my version of that recipe.

50 minutes | Serves 4

Ingredients

– 150g red lentils
– 1 large onion, peeled and diced
– 2 carrots, peeled and diced
– 1 celery stalk, ends removed and diced
– 2 garlic cloves, peeled and finely chopped
– 3-4 sprigs of thyme (or 1 tsp dried)
– 2 x 400g cans tomatoes, chopped or plum
– 3 tsp tomato purée
– 2 tsp gravy granules
– 175ml red wine – or 150ml gravy made with gravy granules
– 10 large mushrooms, sliced
– 1 tbsp olive oil
– A pinch of chilli flakes (optional)
– 3 bay leaves
– 300g spaghetti
– Nutmeg

Heat the oil over a medium heat in a large pan. Fry the onion and garlic for 5 minutes, then add the bay leaves, carrots, celery and lentils and stir well. Cook for another 5 minutes then add the mushrooms, tinned tomatoes, tomato purée, gravy granules and chilli flakes. Place a lid on the pan and simmer over a low heat for 20 minutes, stirring occasionally. Add the wine or gravy, stir well then cook for another 15-20 minutes. Keep stirring and add more liquid if needed.

Boil a pan of salted water and cook the spaghetti for 8-10 minutes, then drain. Grate over some nutmeg and serve with the bolognese sauce on top.

Satay-day night fever

A variation on the theme of Saturday eating – and a pun I'm not afraid to use. If curry's your thing, you'll be dancing around the kitchen when you taste this aubergine and green bean satay which is inspired by a curry that I enjoyed at the Eighth Day Co-operative café in Manchester. Boy, it was good. This is extra special thanks to a hint of galangal, which is part of the ginger family and has a sharp and citrusy flavour. You can find it (fresh and sometimes freeze-dried) in some larger supermarkets and international stores but it's not essential for this curry.

30-35 minutes | Serves 4

Ingredients

- 1 large onion, peeled and diced
- 1 large aubergine, cut into small chunks
- 200g green beans, ends removed
- 200g frozen peas
- 1 x 400ml can coconut milk
- 3 tbsp smooth peanut butter
- 2 tsp galangal
- 2 tsp fresh ginger, peeled and chopped finely
- 2-3 tsp ground cumin
- 1 tsp mustard seeds
- 1 garlic clove, peeled and finely chopped
- The juice of 1 lime
- 1 tbsp coconut oil

In a large pan, heat the oil over a medium heat. Add the onion, garlic, mustard seeds, galangal and ginger and sweat for 5 minutes. Now, add the aubergine, spices, coconut milk, peanut butter and lime juice and bring to the boil. Add the green beans, reduce the heat and simmer for 10-15 minutes. Add the frozen peas and cook for 5 minutes – or until all the vegetables are tender. Serve with rice and poppadums.

Pasta bake

My mum is a great cook but there wasn't always time to make meals from scratch so we often had a pasta bake with a jar of Homepride sauce. I have sweet memories of that creamy sauce, the little shells of pasta and the melted cheese on top.

Fast forward a couple of decades and I've come up with a vegan version which takes a slightly more grown-up approach by using wholewheat pasta, a velvety vegetable sauce and crushed walnuts for a crunchy topping. It may not be the speediest of meals but it's well worth the wait.

1 hour 30 minutes | Serves 4-6

Ingredients

– One large pumpkin or butternut squash
– Half a head of cauliflower broken into florets, and its leaves, chopped coarsely
– 250g wholewheat pasta
– 1 x 400g can tomatoes, chopped or plum
– 2 garlic cloves in their skins
– 3-4 sage leaves, chopped coarsely
– Nutmeg, grated
– Two big handfuls of walnuts, crushed
– Salt and pepper

Preheat the oven to 200C. Slice the pumpkin or squash into wedges (keep the skin and seeds on until later) and place onto a baking sheet (you may need two), then add a little water and season. Place onto the top shelf of the oven and after 20-25 minutes, put the cauliflower onto a separate baking sheet (again, add water and salt and pepper), move the squash to the bottom shelf of the oven, and cook for another 25-30 minutes. In the last ten minutes of cooking, place the whole garlic cloves in with the cauliflower. Remove from the oven and allow to cool.

Cook the pasta in salted water for 8-10 minutes, drain and spread evenly across the base of a large oven dish. Once the pumpkin or squash has cooled, remove the skin and seeds and place in a large bowl with the cauliflower and its leaves. Stir in the tomatoes, half fill the empty can with water then add to the bowl. Stir through the sage and garlic (skins removed) and a generous grating of nutmeg, and blend the mixture in batches. If you don't have a blender, simply put the sauce on a low heat for about 10 minutes and use a wooden spoon to gently crush the cauliflower and pumpkin/squash as you do.

Spread the sauce evenly on top of the pasta. Crush the walnuts and scatter evenly on top of the sauce. Add more nutmeg and salt and pepper, then bake on the top shelf of the oven for 25-30 minutes. Serve with green vegetables – or on its own.

Red lentil and cauliflower tagine with apricot and almond couscous

Disclaimer time: this is more of a stew than an actual tagine but its sweet and spicy taste really lends itself to the well-known Moroccan dish. The cauliflower and lentils make it a filling and Moorish (see what I did there?) meal and it also goes nicely with bread. You can get ras el hanout at most supermarkets and international shops but if you can't find it, you can just use ordinary store cupboard spices.

45-50 minutes | Serves 4

Ingredients

- 1 tbsp olive oil
- 1 small head of cauliflower, cut into florets
- 1 red onion, peeled and diced
- 200g red lentils
- 1 x 400g can tomatoes, chopped or plum
- 2 tsp ras el hanout (or ½ tsp cinnamon, ½ tsp cumin, ½ tsp ginger, ½ tsp coriander)
- 2tsp harissa paste
- 1 tsp fresh ginger, peeled and chopped finely
- 2 garlic cloves, peeled and chopped finely
- 600ml vegetable stock

For the couscous

200g giant couscous
50g dried apricots, chopped
50g flaked almonds
1 tbsp olive oil
1 tsp vegetable stock powder
The juice of 1 lemon
Flat leaf parsley

In a large pan, heat the oil, garlic and ginger over a low to medium heat and fry for 5 minutes. Add the ras el hanout, cauliflower, lentils and carrots and fry for another 5 minutes. Add the stock, tinned tomatoes, tomato purée and harissa paste and stir. Bring to the boil, then reduce the heat, cover the pan with a lid and simmer for 20-25 minutes, stirring occasionally.

Meanwhile, make the couscous. Boil the couscous for 8-10 minutes (or follow packet instructions) then drain and place into a large bowl. Stir through all the ingredients, including the lemon juice then serve with the tagine and the parsley.

Roast cauliflower with all the trimmings

Nothing says Sunday like a roast dinner and you shouldn't have to miss out if you don't eat meat. From time to time, I'll make a nut roast (see my recipe on page 139) but I usually plump for something a bit lighter – after all, I know that I'll always eat far too many roast potatoes – so instead I like to roast a whole cauliflower with all the trimmings. Roasting everything in the same tray means that everything takes on the lovely lemony and garlicky flavours.

The roasted beetroot here is optional but it will provide you with a pleasingly purple gravy. Alternatively, you can just make gravy using the shallots and leftover potato water. If this all sounds like a military operation, don't be put off – just make sure you get someone else to do the washing up.

1 hour 40 minutes | Serves 2-3 (increase the quantities for more people)

Ingredients

– 1 large cauliflower, whole
– 15 baby new potatoes
– 5-6 small carrots, scrubbed and cut into large chunks – or left whole
– 6 shallots (or 2 red or white onions) peeled and halved
– 6 garlic cloves
– 2 unwaxed (if possible, but not essential) lemons, cut into quarters
– 4 tbsp olive oil
– A few sprigs of thyme and/or rosemary (or 1 tsp of each of using dried)
– Salt and pepper

For the lemony crumb topping

– 2-3 handfuls of pine nuts
– The juice of 2 lemons
– 2 garlic cloves, peeled and chopped
– 2 tbsp olive oil

For the roasted beetroot

– 7-8 beetroot, scrubbed and cut into halves
– 2 apples, cored and sliced
– 1 pear, sliced
– 1 tbsp olive oil
– Salt and pepper

For the beetroot gravy

- 1 apple, sliced
- 2 tsp plain flour
- 1 tsp Marmite
- 1 tsp white miso paste (if you don't have this, substitute with 1 tsp Marmite)
- 1 tsp caster sugar
- The leftover water from the beetroot, plus extra water
- A glug of red wine (optional)

If you're not roasting beetroot, make this gravy instead:

- 1 tbsp Marmite
- 1 tbsp plain flour
- 400ml water
- A glug of red wine (optional)

Preheat the oven to 200C and bring two large pans of salted water to the boil. In one, put the cauliflower and in the other, the potatoes, and parboil for 15-20 minutes – after 10 minutes, add the carrots to the pan with the potatoes. In a large ovenproof dish, pour in 2 tbsp olive oil, making sure that the base is fully coated. Remove the cauliflower from the water using a slotted spoon and place in the middle of the dish. Do the same with the potatoes and carrots and place around the cauliflower. Keep the vegetable water if you want to make gravy. Add the shallots and garlic cloves to the pan, then squeeze over the juice from the lemons and leave them in the pan to roast. Sprinkle over the herbs and drizzle over the rest of the olive oil and season with salt and pepper then place on the top shelf of the oven and roast for about an hour, turning the potatoes halfway through. In the last 10 minutes, make the lemony crumb topping by mixing everything in a blender until you have a pesto-like consistency (or use a pestle and mortar to make a rougher paste) then spread liberally over the cauliflower and return to the oven.

Meanwhile, bring another pan of water to the boil and parboil the beetroot for 10 minutes. Remove the beetroot from the pan with a slotted spoon (keep the water in the pan) and put it in an ovenproof dish with the apple and pear and a drizzle of olive oil. Place at the bottom the oven and roast for 40-45 minutes.

Once everything is cooked, cover the dishes while you make the gravy. for the purple gravy, put the pan containing the beetroot water on a low heat and add the flour and the other ingredients, stirring continuously. Remove the skins from two of the garlic cloves and two of the shallots and stir. Add more water if it becomes too thick. Bring to the boil, simmer for 5 minutes and then use a sieve to drain.

If making the other gravy, remove the skins from two of the garlic cloves and two of the shallots then placed in a pan and mix with 200ml of the potato water and 200ml of the cauliflower water plus the Marmite and flour. Mix well, adding the wine, if using, then bring to the boil, simmer for 5 minutes then drain.

Remove the lemons from the oven dish with the cauliflower and serve with green vegetables and whichever gravy you're using.

Highdays and holidays

These are showstopper recipes for special occasions, like birthdays and Christmas – times when you really want to treat yourself or the ones you love. There are also some things that remind me of the food I've eaten on holiday.

Ratatouille

This is a French dish but it actually reminds me of being on holiday in Spain. In a country where you'll often find a tuna salad described as vegetarian, ratatouille (and my other favourite, pan con tomate) is a failsafe option when dining out, and luckily it's also delicious. Apart from its mellifluous name, what I love most about this Mediterranean dish is its simplicity. Chop up the vegetables, chuck them in a pan and leave to cook. It's incredibly versatile, too: eat it with bread, pasta, rice, couscous, vegetables, or just on its own. If you want to bulk it up, serve with some chickpeas or lentils on the side.

1 hour | Serves 4

Ingredients

1 large red or white onion, peeled and cut into small wedges
2 garlic cloves, peeled and finely chopped
1 large aubergine, roughly chopped into small chunks
2 large courgettes, roughly chopped into small chunks
3 red or yellow peppers, roughly chopped into small chunks
6 ripe tomatoes
½ a bunch of fresh basil
2 tbsp olive oil
A few sprigs of fresh thyme
2 x 400g cans tomatoes, chopped or plum
125ml red wine (optional)
1 tablespoon balsamic vinegar (or 3 if not using wine)
2 tbsp olive oil

Heat the oil in a large casserole pan or saucepan over a medium heat, add the chopped aubergines, courgettes and peppers (you may need to do this in batches) and fry for around 5 minutes, or until golden and softened, but not cooked through. Spoon the cooked vegetables into a large bowl.

To the pan, add the onion, garlic, basil stalks and thyme leaves with another drizzle of oil, if needed. Fry for 10 to 15 minutes, or until softened and golden.

Return the cooked vegetables to the pan and stir in the fresh and tinned tomatoes, the balsamic (plus a splash of red wine if you have some going spare) and a good pinch of sea salt and black pepper.

Mix well, breaking up the tomatoes with the back of a spoon. Cover the pan and simmer over a low heat for 30 to 35 minutes, or until it's sticky and sweet.

Tear in the basil leaves and adjust the seasoning, if needed.

Pan con tomate

I'd eat this for every meal if I could – and when I've been on sunny soujourns to Spain, that's pretty much what I've done. Sometimes the simplest dishes are the most delicious and pan con tomate (bread with tomato) is no exception. Buy some nice bread and if you can, tomatoes that are in season (only because they taste nicer), but whatever kind you have, make sure they're at room temperature. This is great for breakfast, as part of a big tapas spread or as a little something to soak up a glass of wine.

Serves 4

Ingredients

– 1 loaf ciabatta or sourdough, sliced as thinly or thickly as you like
– About 10 large tomatoes
– 6 garlic cloves, peeled and bruised
– Extra virgin olive oil
– Sea salt

Toast the bread under the grill. Slice the tops off the tomatoes, making sure to remove the hard stalky bit. Using a box grater, grate the tomatoes into a bowl. Drizzle with olive oil and scatter over some salt. Take the toasted bread and rub with the garlic cloves. Then spread over the tomato mixture, drizzle with oil and sprinkle over some more salt.

Beetroot bourguignon

I've been to Paris twice, although I don't think I ever ate beef bourguignon there. I was probably too busy drinking red wine and practising my A Level French, which is rusty at best these days. I tried this veggie version a couple of years ago at Chapter, a popular arts centre and café bar in Cardiff, and fell in love with it. Here's my take on that delicious dish – I've added apples for a sweet balance to the earthiness of the beetroot. This is a dream served with creamy mashed potato and garlicky green beans.

1 hour | Serves 4

Ingredients

- 8 small beetroot, peeled and roughly sliced (or use 2 packs of the vacuum-packed variety)
- 400g green lentils, rinsed and drained
- 2 onions (or 4 shallots), peeled and finely chopped
- 2 garlic cloves, peeled and finely sliced
- 4 carrots, peeled and chopped into medium-sized chunks
- 2 parsnips, peeled and chopped into medium-sized chunks
- 2 apples, cored and chopped into medium-sized chunks
- 8 medium-sized mushrooms, sliced
- 4 tbsp tomato purée
- 2 tsp plain flour
- 250ml red wine (or vegetable stock)
- 1 litre vegetable stock
- 2 tbsp olive oil
- 3 bay leaves
- 4 sprigs of thyme

Heat 1 tbsp oil in a large pan over a medium heat. Add the onions and garlic and sauté for five minutes until soft. Add the beetroot, apple, parsnips, carrots and bay leaves and season with salt and pepper. Cook for 5 minutes, stirring frequently.

Stir in the tomato purée, red wine and stock, then add the lentils. Bring to the boil, then reduce the heat, cover the pan with a lid and simmer for 30 minutes.

Meanwhile, heat a frying pan, add 1 tbsp oil and sear the mushrooms until golden brown. Season and set aside.

Taste the stew and add more wine, stock or herbs if needed. Add the flour and stir, then add the mushrooms and simmer for another 10 minutes. Remove the bay leaves and thyme sprigs before serving.

Tacos with pulled jackfruit

Pulled pork is still all the rage and no longer is it found exclusively at hipster pop-up restaurants. Happily, now that eating plants is pretty cool, some clever cooks have discovered that jackfruit, when prepared properly, has a pretty similar texture to meat – who'd have thought it? Don't be put off by that if you're not a flesh fan though – it sounds weird but jackfruit just works.

These tacos are deliciously moreish and pretty easy to make, too. You should be able to find jackfruit in international food shops, but if you come away empty-handed you can use refried beans, or even chickpeas – just mash them up a bit first.

20-25 minutes | Serves 4 – three tacos per person

Ingredients

– 2 x 400g cans jackfruit in brine
– 1 medium onion, sliced into thin slices
– 2 garlic cloves
– 1 tsp cinnamon
– 2 ½ tbsp. maple syrup
– The juice of 1 lime
– 1 tsp smoked paprika
– ½ tsp chilli powder
– 150ml water
– 1 tbsp olive oil
– 1 packet of tacos

Rinse the jackfruit thoroughly, then drain and rub it between your fingers until it breaks apart and becomes stringy. Don't throw away the edible stems and seeds – chop them up and add to rest of the fruit. Over a medium heat, fry the onions and garlic in the olive oil for about 5 minutes, or until they are browned. Add the jackfruit, the water, maple syrup, lime juice and spices and stir. Add the water, stir, cover with a lid, then simmer for 15 minutes, stirring occasionally.

Heat the oven to 180C and place the taco shells on a large baking tray. Bake for 3-4 minutes, or according to packet instructions. Then simply fill each taco shell with some pulled jackfruit. Serve with guacamole (see recipe on page 98), vegan yogurt or soured cream, coriander and lime wedges.

Kentucky Fried Cauliflower (KFC) with sweet potato fries

I've actually never been to this popular fast food restaurant; it just wasn't somewhere we went as kids, probably because we didn't eat that much meat. I won't lie and pretend that I don't think crispy fried chicken tastes good (because it does) but it's off the menu for me now. Anyway, when you try this deep-fried cauliflower, you'll soon realise that it's just as delicious and best of all, cruelty-free. It's surprisingly easy to make (although expect a bit of mess when you're frying) and uses most of the 'secret' spice blend used by KFC. By grounding the flaxseed, you create an egg-like binder which makes the spicy coating stick to the cauliflower.

There's no other way to say this: these are delicious. Seriously good and definitely worth the mess. Deep frying is strangely meditative, too.

45 minutes | Serves 2

Ingredients

– 1 large head of cauliflower, cut into largish pieces
– 200ml vegetable oil, or more depending on how shallow your pan is

For the dry coating

– 3 tsp salt
– ½ tsp dried thyme
– ½ tsp dried basil
– ½ tsp dried oregano
– 2 tsp black pepper
– 2 tsp sweet paprika
– 2 tsp smoked paprika
– 1 tsp ground ginger
– 2 tsp brown sugar
– 150g plain flour

For the wet coating

– 2 tbsp ground flaxseed (or linseed) or chia seeds
– 3 tbsp hot sauce
– 1 tbsp Dijon mustard
– 1 tbsp maple syrup
– 70ml water

For the sweet potato fries

– 2 large sweet potatoes, peeled and sliced very thinly
– 1 tbp olive oil
– 1 tsp smoked paprika
– ½ tsp dried rosemary or thyme
– 1-2 tbsp plain flour or cornflour
– Salt and pepper

Preheat the oven to 200C. Make the chips by popping everything into a freezer bag and shaking it so that the potato fries are coated. Place them onto greaseproof paper on a baking sheet and roast for 20-25 minutes.

Meanwhile, make the wet coating for your cauliflower. Put the seeds into a food processor or grind in a pestle and mortar. Add to a bowl and mix together with the other ingredients. Stir well and give it a few minutes to thicken.

Make your dry coating. In a large bowl, mix the flour with all the spices, sugar and salt and pepper.

Pour the vegetable oil into a large pan (make sure it's about 2-3cm high so that the cauliflower pieces are fully submerged when you dip them in) and place on a high heat. Make sure that it doesn't get too hot – it shouldn't bubble or splatter.

Now comes the messy bit. Take a cauliflower piece and dip it into the wet coating, making sure to cover both sides. Dip into the flour coating, again covering both sides. Now, repeat the process: roll in the wet coating and then again in the flour mixture.

Using tongs, take the cauliflower and submerge in the oil. Cook for 4-5 minutes, turning occasionally, until brown and crispy. Place on a plate with some kitchen roll to absorb some of the oil. Repeat with all the pieces (you may need to top up the oil), then serve with the sweet potato fries.

Maple-roasted sprouts with pecans and cranberries

E ven as a seven-year-old, my favourite vegetable was, and still is, the much scorned sprout. I have never understood why people hate them so much. Maybe it's down to over boiling or because, let's be honest, they're not much to look at it. Whatever it is, I want to reclaim sprouts because, cooked properly, they can be absolutely delicious.

If you're still in doubt, try roasting them instead. With this recipe, you deck the sprouts with crunchy pecans and tangy cranberries and add a hint of sweetness by roasting them all in maple syrup. You'll be surprised by how good this tastes – and so will everyone else at the table.

50-55 minutes | Serves 4-6

Ingredients

– 350g sprouts
– 75g pecans
– 50g dried cranberries
– 2 tbsp olive oil
– 3 tbsp maple syrup
– 1 tbsp apple cider vinegar
– 2 tsp cinnamon

Preheat the oven to 200C. In a large bowl, mix the oil, maple syrup, vinegar and cinnamon. Cut off the end of the sprouts and the immediate outer leaves. Slice in half, add to the bowl and mix thoroughly so that the sprouts are all coated in the maple dressing. Place in an oven dish and roast for 20 minutes. Remove from the oven and add the pecans and the cranberries and cook for another 10 minutes.

Strawberry cheesecake

Now this is what I call indulgent. Forget everything you've read about raw cheesecake because this is the complete opposite of anything that so-called clean eaters would let pass their lips. My favourite pudding when I was growing up was definitely strawberry cheesecake which Mum would sometimes pop in the shopping trolley if we'd been on our best behaviour. If you like sweet stuff, you'll love this veganised version. I use strawberry jam (my favourite is Bonne Maman) but use the fresh ones when they're in season if you want a slightly more grown-up version. A lot of the cheaper or value brand digestive biscuits are vegan but check the label.

25-30 minutes, plus chilling time | Serves 6-8

Ingredients

– For the biscuit base
– 200g vegan digestive biscuits
– 100g dairy-free margarine

For the topping

– 300g plain vegan cream cheese at room temperature
– 150g soya or dairy-free yogurt
– 100g icing sugar
– 1 jar (370g) strawberry jam

Grease a springform cake tin or flan dish. In a bowl, crush the digestive biscuits with a rolling pin. Melt the margarine in a pan, then pour it over the digestive biscuit crumbs. Mix thoroughly, and pour into the cake tin. Press down evenly with a spoon until the base is very firmly compacted. Push the crumb base up to the edges a little so that it comes off the base more easily if you're using a springform tin.

Put the yogurt, cream cheese and icing sugar in a food processor and blend until smooth. Alternatively, you can use a whisk or a fork, although this will require a bit of elbow grease! Pour the topping over the biscuit base and chill in the fridge for at least 8 hours or overnight, preferably. When it's set, spoon over the strawberry jam, making sure to spread it evenly, or top with fresh strawberries. Serve immediately. This will keep in the fridge for a couple of days, although it probably won't last that long...

Caesar salad with a twist of Waldorf

When I was a teenager, I became a lot more tuned in to what I thought was healthy eating and when we went to restaurants, I'd order a chicken Caesar salad because to me, it seemed the height of sophistication – and because I loved the crunchy croutons. It never really left me feeling very satisfied though, and I'd always need pudding afterwards.

My vegan version of this classic salad is so much tastier than anything I ate back in those days and the apple and walnuts give it a twist of Waldorf, too. Not all salads are made equal, and although it contains lettuce, this is definitely not one for the dieters, but the creamy cashew dressing is sheer heaven. Serve it at a dinner or picnic and I can guarantee that everyone will want seconds. It goes particularly well with the porkless pie on page 145.

45 minutes | Serves 2

Ingredients

For the salad

– 1 x 400g can chickpeas, rinsed and drained
– 200g stale bread, cut into small chunks
– 6 tbsp olive oil
– 2 tbsp white wine vinegar
– The juice of 1 lemon
– 1 head of romaine lettuce, roughly chopped
– 4-5 leaves of kale, roughly chopped (or half a bag of ready prepared)
– 1 apple, cored and sliced into segments
– 50 g walnuts, roughly chopped
– Salt and pepper

For the creamy dressing

– 100g cashews, soaked for 3 hours or overnight then drained
– 2 garlic cloves, peeled and finely chopped
– 2 tbsp capers, plus a little brine from the jar
– The juice of half a lemon
– 3 tbsp olive oil
– 1 tsp Dijon mustard
– 3-4 tbsp water
– 1 tbsp nutritional yeast flakes
– Salt and pepper.

Preheat the oven to 200C. In a bowl, combine the chickpeas and bread with 4 tbsp olive oil and season with salt and pepper. Layer evenly in an ovenproof dish, place on the top shelf of the oven and bake for 20-25 minutes. In the bowl which had the chickpeas and bread, massage the kale with 2 tbsp olive oil, half the lemon juice and some salt and pepper. Spread across a large oven tray or dish and bake for 5 minutes. When cooked, remove from the oven and allow to cool for 5 minutes.

Meanwhile, make the dressing. Blend the cashews, garlic, capers and lemon juice in a food processor then add the olive oil, water and mustard and blend again until you have a creamy consistency. Taste, add the nutritional yeast flakes and some salt and pepper, then pour into a bowl and set aside to thicken slightly. If you don't have a food processor, you can mash the softened cashews in a pestle and mortar (or using the base of a mug) and then whisk all the ingredients together in a bowl.

In a large bowl, add the lettuce and apple and massage with the rest of the lemon juice. Add the chickpeas, croutons and kale and combine. Serve with the creamy dressing and sprinkle over the chopped walnuts. If you're eating this away from home (or at a picnic) keep the dressing in a separate container and pour over just before eating.

Christmassy chestnut and cranberry roast

Sure, Christmas has been done to death but I still love it. When else do you get time off work to lounge around, watch telly and drink fizz at 9am? Festive food is rather different as a vegan, though: goodbye to turkey, cheeseboards and pigs in blankets; hello, dark chocolate, figs and that old chestnut, the nut roast.

My friend Avis has been vegetarian for most of her life but she has some pretty strong opinions about nut roasts which she refuses to eat. I'll admit that in the past, I too have been dismissive of the old nut roast because it can be dry and flavourless, but I promise you that this one, which uses chestnuts, lentils, cranberries and apricots, isn't. It's a doddle to make and can be assembled on Christmas Eve if needs be.

Serve with roasted root vegetables, red cabbage, and my recipe for maple and cinnamon roasted sprouts with pecans and cranberries on page 133.

1 hour 30, plus cooling time | Serves 4-6

Ingredients

- 100g chestnuts, chopped
- 50g dried cranberries
- 30g dried apricots
- 2 x 400g cans lentils
- 1 large carrot, grated
- 2 apples, grated
- 2 stalks celery, finely chopped
- 3 shallots or one large onion, peeled and diced
- 2 garlic cloves, peeled and finely chopped
- 2 tsp fresh thyme
- 1 tbsp balsamic vinegar
- 2 tbsp maple syrup
- 2 tbsp olive oil

Preheat the oven to 180C. Grease a 9×5 inch loaf pan, and then line it with a piece of greaseproof paper cut to fit the length of the pan. Rinse and drain the lentils in a colander then pour them into a large bowl and mash with a potato masher. The aim here is to create a lentil paste while still leaving about one third of the lentils intact.

Add the oil into a large pan, and increase the heat to medium. Stir in the shallots, or onion, and garlic and season with a pinch or two of salt. Cook for 4-5 minutes until the onion softens.

Stir in the celery and carrot, and continue cooking for another few minutes. Now stir in the grated apple, dried cranberries and apricots, thyme, a generous pinch of salt and some black pepper. Cook for a few more minutes.

Stir the chestnuts into the mashed lentils mixture and add the balsamic vinegar and maple syrup, then stir in all of the veggie mixture until combined. If the mixture seems dry, add a tablespoon or two of water and mix again.

Press all of the lentil loaf mixture into the prepared loaf pan. Pack it down as firmly as you can as this will help it hold together after cooling.

Bake the lentil loaf uncovered for 45-50 minutes until the edges start to darken and the loaf is semi-firm to the touch. Place the loaf pan directly onto a cooling rack for 15 minutes. Then, slide a knife around the ends to loosen, and carefully lift out the loaf (using the parchment paper as "handles") and place it directly onto the cooling rack for another 30 minutes.

After cooling, carefully slice the loaf into slabs. Serve immediately. The loaf will continue to firm up as it cools. Some crumbling is normal if sliced while warm.

Carrot cake

The humble carrot cake's not as wholesome as you'd think and made the right way it can be very, very decadent. I remember eating big wedges of it at Crumbs in Cardiff and if we went to London, Cranks, the world-famous vegetarian restaurant, which has now sadly closed.

These days, this teatime favourite is more hip than hippy – and if you're put off by the thought of carrots in a cake, don't be; they add a hint of sweetness and give a lovely, moist texture. In fact, the carrots were used to substitute butter and sugar when they were rationed during the war and a big slice of this will please even the sweetest tooth.

When I was a kid, I loved the little icing carrots that used to decorate carrot cakes, but I'm all fingers and thumbs with arts and crafts and have never been able to do them justice. Don't worry about making a bit of a mess with the icing – it's not The Great British Bake Off, after all.

1 hour | Serves 6-8

Ingredients

– 100ml sunflower oil, plus extra for greasing
– 230g self-raising flour
– 1 tsp baking powder
– 1½ tsp ground cinnamon
– ½ tsp allspice
– ½ tsp ground ginger
– 200g light brown muscovado sugar
– The juice of 1 orange
– 75g pecans, halved, plus extra for decorating
– 300g carrots, coarsely grated
– 1 large apple, coarsely grated
– 100g sultanas

For the icing

– 100g vegan margarine, softened
– 200g vegan cream cheese, at room temperature
– 100g icing sugar, plus extra to dust
– Finely grated zest of 1 orange

Preheat the oven to 180°C. Grease two 18cm loose-bottomed round sandwich cake tins and line the base with baking paper. Sift the flour, baking powder and spices into a large bowl. Add the sugar, orange juice, pecans, sultanas and grated carrots and apple, then stir until well combined. Stir in the oil, then mix well.

Pour into the prepared cake tins and bake in the oven for 40-45 minutes or until a skewer comes out clean. Transfer to a cooling rack, leave in the tins for 5 minutes, then turn out and leave to cool completely before icing.

To make the icing, simply beat together the margarine and cream cheese. Sieve over the icing sugar then beat again – try to make sure that there are no lumps. When you're ready to ice the cake, place one of the sponges onto a plate, spread over a thick layer of icing, then place the second sponge on top. Spread over the icing and decorate with the pecans plus some orange zest, if you like. To store, keep in a cake tin in the fridge for 2-3 days.

Porkless pie

As a kid, I treated a pork pie with a certain kind of reverence usually reserved for Father Christmas and later on, Leonardo DiCaprio. I thought it a real work of art: all that golden, buttery pastry and perfectly pink pork. We used to eat pork pie for a picnic, often at St Fagans or the museum in town, and on Boxing Day with cold turkey and salad.

This meat-free version uses tofu as the 'meat' which is firm and flavoursome thanks to the herby marinade. The hot crust pastry is surprisingly easy to make even if, like me, you're a bit of a novice in that department. Enjoy it hot or cold, with piccalilli or fruit chutney.

2 hours | Serves 4-6

Ingredients

For the filling
- 1½ x 400g blocks firm tofu
- 3 tbsp olive oil
- 1 tsp vegetable stock powder
- ½ tsp ground thyme
- ½ tsp ground rosemary
- The juice of 1 lemon

For the pastry
- 350 g plain flour
- 1 tsp baking powder
- 100 g vegan margarine or vegetable fat
- 175 ml water
- 1 tsp salt
- Some plant milk or vegan margarine for glazing

Take the tofu and use kitchen roll or a clean tea towel to blot and absorb all its water. Take two heavy wooden chopping boards and place on either side of the blocks to 'press' it and absorb excess moisture. If you can, put something heavy, like a hardback book, on top of the chopping board to weigh it down further. Leave for at least 30 minutes then make your marinade. In a shallow dish, mix together the olive oil, the stock powder, herbs and the lemon juice, then slice the tofu blocks in half lengthways and place the slabs into the dish, making sure to coat all sides. Season with salt and pepper and leave for 30 minutes to an hour.

Preheat the oven to 200C, bake for 15-20 minutes, then, keeping the oven switched on, take out and set aside. To make the pastry, sieve the flour, baking powder and salt into a large bowl and mix. In a pan, heat the vegetable fat and water until it comes to the boil, then pour into the flour mixture and mix. When it has cooled, form the mixture into a large dough ball (if you think it's a bit dry, add a few drops of water, but no more or it will become tacky) and divide in half. Take one half, roll onto a floured surface and place at the base of a greased springform cake tin or pie dish – use one that's about 10 inches in diameter. On top of this, place the tofu slabs and season with salt and pepper. Now, roll out the rest of the pastry, making it a bit bigger than the pastry base so that it can fold over the top and use this to cover the pie filling. Try to do it as neatly as possible and make sure that there are no gaps or holes for the filling to come through. Use your fingers to seal the pastry then brush over a little milk or margarine and place on the top shelf of the oven and bake for 30 minutes or until golden brown.

Chestnut and sundried tomato casserole

This casserole is one of the best things I've ever tasted and can be enjoyed at any time of the year. It's a winter warmer when eaten with red cabbage and a glass of red wine. In the summer, serve with crusty bread, green vegetables and crisp, dry white wine.

If you can't find chestnuts (or don't like nuts), use two cans of chickpeas instead.

1 hour | Serves 4

Ingredients

For the casserole

- 1 tablespoon olive oil
- 1 large onion, peeled and diced
- 2 carrots, peeled and chopped into small chunks
- 2 celery sticks, ends removed and diced
- 2 garlic cloves, peeled and finely chopped
- 200g cooked chestnuts (use the vacuum-packed variety if you like), halved roughly
- ½ a 285g jar sundried tomatoes, drained of oil and torn
- 2 apples, cored and cut into small chunks
- 1 tsp fresh rosemary, chopped
- 2 tsp fresh thyme, chopped
- 2 x 400g cans tomatoes, chopped or plum
- 2 tsp tomato purée
- 1 tsp Marmite
- 2 handfuls of kale, stalks removed

For the topping

- 2 medium sweet potatoes, peeled and cut into small chunks
- 1 tsp ground cinnamon
- A liberal sprinkling of nutmeg
- 1 tsp maple syrup
- A pinch of sea salt and pepper
- 1 tbsp coconut oil, melted (use olive oil if you prefer)
- 2 handfuls of pecans

In a pan, heat the olive oil and onion over a medium heat and cook for 2 minutes. Add the carrot, celery and garlic and cook for a further 2 minutes until the vegetables are starting to soften.

Add the chestnuts, sundried tomato, apple, rosemary and thyme then pour in the chopped tomatoes and the tomato purée. Spoon in the Marmite and stir thoroughly. Place a lid on the pan, reduce the heat to low medium and cook for 20 minutes, stirring occasionally.

Meanwhile, peel and slice the sweet potato and boil for 15-20 minutes. Add the maple syrup, cinnamon, coconut oil and nutmeg and mash, then set aside.

Heat the oven to 200C. Add the kale to the casserole mixture, stir through and cook for a further 10 minutes until the kale has wilted. Season with sea salt and pepper to taste. If your pan isn't oven proof, transfer the mixture to a casserole or oven dish and top with a layer of mashed potato. Grate over the nutmeg, add the chopped pecans and another liberal sprinkling of cinnamon.

Place a lid on the casserole (or if using a dish wrap loosely in foil) and cook for 10-15 minutes until the pecans are slightly toasted.

Gourmet goulash with treacle

This traditional Hungarian dish is named after the herdsmen or cowboys who invented the stew, which makes sense as it normally contains a hefty amount of beef. This vegan version uses pinto beans which makes a rich and hearty stew and the treacle adds a bit of sweetness, too. This is perfect for warming up on a cold night and goes very well with a glass of red wine. I like to eat mine with a little sauerkraut, although that's not to everyone's taste.

45 minutes | Serves 4

Ingredients

- 1 tbsp olive oil
- 2 shallots, peeled and finely chopped
- 1 green pepper, sliced into thin strips
- 1 small carrot, diced
- 1 celery stalk, stalks removed and diced
- 3 garlic cloves (use the smoked variety if you can), peeled and finely chopped
- ½ tsp caraway seeds
- 1 tsp smoked paprika
- 1 tsp sweet paprika
- 1 x 400g can tomatoes, chopped or plum
- 1 x 400g can pinto beans or any other kind of canned beans, rinsed and drained
- 2 heaped tbsp treacle
- A glug of red wine (optional)
- 2 tsp tomato purée
- 4 large leaves of savoy cabbage, shredded
- Salt and pepper

Preheat the oven to 180C. Heat the oil over a medium heat in a large pan or casserole. Add the onion, carrot and celery and let them sweat for five minutes then add the garlic, caraway seeds, both types of paprika and the sliced pepper. Season with salt and pepper. Cook for 2 minutes then add the tinned tomato. Fill the empty can with water and add to the pan, then stir through the treacle, wine (if using) and tomato purée. Bring to the boil, then reduce the heat and add the beans and cabbage. Cook for 5 minutes then transfer to an ovenproof dish (if you're not using a casserole that's flame-proof) and cook for 20 minutes. If you'd prefer, you can keep cooking the goulash on the hob over a low heat with the lid on for another 20 minutes.

Serve with rice or potatoes and some vegan yogurt and parsley.

Chocolate and chestnut puddings

I think of this as an alternative to traditional Christmas pudding, even though you can enjoy it at any time of year. These surprisingly simple little puds are densely chocolatey, melt in the middle and are just divine with vegan ice cream or crème fraiche. If you don't like chestnuts, leave them out, but they do add a richer taste and texture.

25-30 minutes | Serves 4

Ingredients

– 200g dark chocolate, broken into small pieces
– 1 tbsp coconut oil
– 200ml plant milk
– 150g self-raising flour
– 100g caster sugar
– 100g chestnut purée
– 1 tsp ground cinnamon

Preheat the oven to 200C. Carefully place a heatproof bowl over a pan of boiling water and add the chocolate and coconut oil and stir gently until melted. Remove the bowl from the pan and set aside to cool slightly. If you have a microwave, heat the bowl on a medium power at 60-second intervals until melted. When the chocolate mixture has cooled slightly stir through the chestnut purée then add the milk and whisk. Fold in the flour and sugar until combined and stir thoroughly. Pour into ramekins and bake in the oven for 10 minutes. You'll know it's ready when the top is shiny and cracks slightly.

Comfort food and childhood favourites

This is comfort food, pure and simple and the equivalent of a big old cwtch. Traditional favourites like cawl and bara brith are the food of the Gods in Wales so I've included them here as well as other classics like lasagne, tomato soup and chocolate brownies. This is the stuff to eat when you're feeling poorly, need cheering up or if you have a raging hangover.

Tomato soup

They say that chicken soup is good for the soul but even when I ate meat, I hated the stuff. In times of trouble I always turned to Heinz tomato soup but now I make my own. Most shop-bought soups can contain a lot of sugar and salt and besides, homemade costs a fraction of the price.

This recipe takes no time at all to make, is s(o)uper easy and uses just three main ingredients: tomatoes, onions and olive oil. The best bit is that there is minimal chopping and you can even use tinned tomatoes if you're really rushed for time.

If you're not a chilli fiend like me, try using fresh or dried basil or oregano.

45 minutes | Serves 4

Ingredients

– 12-13 large tomatoes, roughly cut into small wedges – make sure to remove the hard part at the top – or 2 x 400g tins cans tomatoes, chopped or plum
– 2 onions (red or white), peeled and diced
– 2-3 tbsp olive oil
– 1 chilli (optional), finely chopped
– 2 garlic cloves, peeled and finely chopped
– ½ tsp dried basil
– 1 litre water
– Salt and pepper

Heat the oil over a medium heat in a large pan or saucepan. Add the onions and garlic and fry for 5 minutes, then add the water, tomatoes, basil and chilli, if you're using it. Season with salt and pepper. Bring to the boil then cover, reduce the heat and simmer for 30 minutes. Stir occasionally and add additional salt as needed.

Turn off the heat and leave to cool for 5-10 minutes. Now blend the soup using a hand-held blender or a regular one. If you're using the latter, it's best to blend in batches and not fill the blender as much as you usually would since the soup is so hot. Return to the pan and reheat. Serve with bread or on its own.

Lasagne

Lasagne always makes me think of those old Dolmio adverts from the 1990s, where a large Italian family would congregate over a huge dish of pasta. This meat-free lasagne is much nicer than the ready-made versions so popular back then and although it takes a little time to make, it's surprisingly straightforward and the taste is molto bueno; in fact, the béchamel sauce is so creamy that you'd never guess that it's dairy free.

1 hour 15 minutes | Serves 4

Ingredients

For the ragu

- 200g green or red lentils
- 2 x 400g cans tomatoes, chopped or plum
- 1 large onion, peeled and diced
- 2 garlic cloves, peeled and chopped finely
- 1 celery stalk, stalks removed and diced
- 1 large carrot, diced
- 1 tsp dried rosemary
- 4–5 tsp tomato purée
- 1 tbsp olive oil
- 2 tbsp balsamic vinegar
- 6 dried lasagne sheets (egg-free)
- 100g vegan cheese, grated (optional)

For the béchamel sauce

- 700ml soya, nut or oat milk
- 2 bay leaves
- 1 onion, peeled and roughly sliced
- 6 tbsp plain flour
- 2 tbsp olive oil
- 1½ tsp vegetable stock powder
- ¼ tsp nutmeg, grated
- Salt and black pepper

First of all, make the ragu sauce. In a large pan, heat the oil over a low to medium heat, then add the onions and garlic and fry for 5 minutes. Now add the carrot, celery, lentils, tomatoes (plus fill one of the empty cans with water and pour into the pan), tomato purée, balsamic vinegar and rosemary. Reduce the heat, cover the pan with a lid and simmer for 30 minutes, stirring occasionally.

While the ragu is cooking, make your béchamel sauce. Place all the ingredients, except for the oil and flour, into a saucepan and mix together. Bring to the boil, then remove from the heat and set aside and allow to cool. Remove the onion and bay leaves using a slotted spoon. In a separate saucepan, mix together the flour and oil until you have a smooth paste. Gradually, pour in the milk mixture, whisking or stirring constantly. Place the pan on a high heat and bring to the boil, whisking or stirring all the time, until the mixture thickens to a smooth sauce. Make it as thick as you like by adding extra flour – or if you want a thinner sauce, add more milk. Season with salt and pepper and remove from the heat.

Preheat the oven to 200C. Take an ovenproof dish and spread over a layer of ragu at the base, followed by a layer of béchamel sauce, then about three lasagne sheets (or more depending on the size of your dish. Repeat the layer of ragu, béchamel and lasagne sheets, then add a final layer of béchamel sauce and scatter over the grated cheese, if using.

Place on the top shelf of the oven and bake for 30 minutes.

Anything goes dahl

Roald Dahl was born just down the road from us in Cardiff (he lived there until the age of twelve) and growing up, I felt a real affinity with Matilda, Charlie, Danny and Sophie – children, who like me, were a bit different. In a world of snozzcumbers, exploding candy and gobstoppers, I fitted in.

Now, dahl (or dhal, depending on how you spell it) as a dish is interesting, too, plus it's nourishing, super speedy to make and if you're feeling the pinch, it'll last you until pay day. It's also a good way to clear the fridge of any vegetables that have been sitting around for a while. You can serve this with rice, bread or just on its own.

25-30 minutes | Serves 3-4

Ingredients

– 1 onion, peeled and finely chopped
– 1 tsp olive oil or coconut oil
– 2 garlic cloves, peeled and finely chopped
– 1½ tsp ginger, peeled and finely grated
– ½ tsp cumin
– ¼ tsp turmeric
– ½ tsp dried coriander
– ½ tsp black mustard seeds
– ¼ tsp curry powder
– 180g red lentils, rinsed well in a sieve under a running tap
– Pinch of salt
– 1 tsp vegetable bouillon powder
– 800ml boiling water
– 1 courgette, grated

First of all, heat the oil in a medium saucepan over a medium heat and soften the onion. When it starts to turn translucent, add the ginger and garlic. Stir well and once they start to release their aroma, add all the spices. Stir well and add a splash of water if they start to catch. After a minute or so, add the lentils and the salt and stir well. Add the vegetable bouillon powder and 500ml boiling water. Cook for about 10 minutes over a medium heat until the lentils turn pale yellow, then add the grated courgette and 300ml more boiling water. Give it another good stir but don't be too vigorous or you'll slop dahl all over yourself.

Simmer over a medium heat for 10 more minutes until the courgette is tender and the lentils are cooked, adding more water if it seems too dry.

Bara brith

This is very much a teatime favourite in Wales. Bara is the Welsh for bread and the brith refers to the speckles of dried fruit in the loaf. It's deep-rooted in Welsh culture but it's also eaten in Argentina, as it was taken over by Welsh settlers who moved there in the late nineteenth century. This is more like cake than bread but it's delicious slathered in butter or vegan margarine. You can use any plant milk for this, but hazelnut milk gives a wonderfully nutty taste to temper the sweetness of the fruit.

1 hour 45 minutes | Makes one large loaf

Ingredients
– 400g dried mixed fruit
– 300ml warm tea
– 400g self-raising flour
– 100g brown sugar
– 1 apple, grated
– 2 tsp mixed spice
– 75ml plant milk
– Oil or vegan margarine for greasing the loaf tin

In a large bowl, pour the warm tea over the dried fruit and leave overnight (or if you're short of time, a few hours will do). Preheat the oven to 170C. Sieve over the flour, then combine with the dried fruit, sugar, mixed spice and apple. Add the milk and stir through. Grease a 9×5 inch loaf tin and pour the cake batter into it, making sure that it's spread evenly. Place on the top shelf of the oven and bake for 1 to 1.5 hours or until a skewer inserted into the middle comes out clean.

Savoury crumble

Crumble is up there on my list of favourite comfort foods and it's easy to see why it's a bit of a national institution. This British classic became popular during the Second World War when pastry ingredients were in short supply as the result of rationing.

Who doesn't love softly stewed fruit, a crunchy topping and lashings of custard? It's nice to have a change once in a while though, which is why I've tinkered with the original recipe to create this savoury version. The woodiness of the mushrooms works well with the buttery topping and I've added some apple for a little sweetness – I wouldn't want to stray too far from tradition after all. Instead of custard or cream, you can enjoy this with a rich gravy and mashed or roast potatoes and peas.

1 hour | Serves 2

Ingredients

For the filling

– 1 tbsp olive oil
– 150g mushrooms, sliced
– 1 large leek, thinly sliced
– 2 apples, cored and diced
– 3-4 sprigs of thyme, stalks removed
– 2 tsp wholegrain mustard
– Salt and pepper

For the crumble topping

– 200g flour
– 150g vegan margarine, cold from the fridge
– 2-3 tbsp nutritional yeast flakes (optional)

For the gravy

– 1 tsp olive oil
– 1 large leek, thinly sliced
– 2 tbsp plain flour
– 200ml hot vegetable stock
– 1 tsp Marmite or miso paste

Preheat the oven to 200C. Heat the oil in a frying pan over a medium heat and sauté the mushrooms, leek and apple with the thyme for about 5 minutes then set aside.

Make the crumble mixture. Sieve the flour into a bowl and, using your fingers, rub in the margarine until you have breadcrumbs.

Stir the mustard through the mushroom mixture and season with salt and pepper. Layer evenly across the base of an ovenproof dish and then top with the crumble mixture. Place on the top shelf of the oven and bake for 35-40 minutes. In the last 10 minutes, remove from the oven and sprinkle over the yeast flakes, if using.

To make the gravy, heat the oil in a pan over a medium heat and sauté the leek for 3-4 minutes or until soft and translucent. Pour in the stock and stir through the flour and Marmite or miso paste. Bring to the boil, then reduce the heat and cook for about 5 minutes, stirring frequently. Pour through a sieve to get rid of the leeks and transfer to a jug or gravy boat. Pour over the crumble and serve immediately.

Cauliflower 'cheese'

I haven't eaten cauliflower cheese since I was a kid but I have fond memories of enjoying this comforting dish, snuggled up on the sofa watching Heartbeat while I avoided doing my homework. This king of comfort food has had a revival in recent years and can now be found on the menu at hip eateries across the country alongside the now almost ubiquitous mac 'n' cheese.

This is perhaps the closest you can get to creamy without using dairy – and the secret ingredient here is the humble cashew nut. It's perfect as a side dish – to accompany a Sunday roast, perhaps – or enjoyed all on its own.

45 minutes, plus soaking time for the cashews | Serves 4-6

Ingredients
– 1 head of cauliflower, broken into florets
– 120g cashew nuts, soaked and drained
– 400ml plant milk
– 1 large onion, peeled and diced
– 2 tbsp flour
– 3 tbsp nutritional yeast flakes
– 3 tsp wholegrain mustard
– The juice of 1 lemon
– 1 tbsp olive oil
– Salt and pepper
– A generous grating of nutmeg (or half a teaspoon if using powder)

Soak the cashews for at least three hours if you can, although an hour will do if you're short of time. Drain and rinse then set aside. Place in a food processor and blend, adding a little plant milk to make sure it doesn't stick to the sides. Boil or steam the cauliflower for 8-10 minutes. Meanwhile, heat the oil in a pan over a medium heat and fry the onions for 5 minutes, or until soft. Preheat the oven to 200C and when the cauliflower is cooked, drain and set aside. In a large pan, combine the plant milk, flour, cashews and mustard and stir vigorously to get rid of any lumps. Add the lemon juice and some salt and pepper and stir, adding a little water if it becomes too thick. Add the nutritional yeast and nutmeg and stir for another minute. Remove the pan from the heat and gently stir through the cauliflower. Layer evenly into a large ovenproof dish and sprinkle over some more yeast flakes and nutmeg, if you like. Place on the top shelf of the oven and bake for 15-20 minutes, or until the top is a light golden brown.

Chocolate orange brownies

These brownies remind me of Christmas when, if you're lucky, it's likely that you'll find a Terry's chocolate orange at the bottom of your stocking. Baking these vegan dark chocolate orange brownies fills the house with the smell of Yuletide and will make even the soberest of Scrooges smile nostalgically. If you can't find orange extract, you can leave it out, but it does give the brownies a more citrusy flavour.

45 minutes | Makes 10-12 brownies

Ingredients

– 200g dark chocolate
– 200g flour
– 2 tsp baking powder
– 1 tsp bicarbonate of soda
– 3 tbsp cocoa powder
– The juice of 2 large oranges
– 2-3 tsp orange extract
– 2 tbsp date/maple syrup
– 300ml almond, soya or oat milk
– Pinch of salt

Preheat the oven to 180C. Place a heatproof bowl over a pan of simmering water, making sure that the base doesn't touch the water. Break the chocolate into the bowl and allow it to melt, then set aside to cool slightly. Alternatively, break the chocolate into small pieces and place into a microwaveable bowl. Heat on medium power at 60-second intervals until melted. Set aside and allow to cool. Sieve the flour, baking powder, bicarbonate of soda and cocoa powder into a large bowl. Add the maple syrup, orange juice, almond milk and a pinch of salt, and stir well. Now, add the melted chocolate and the remainder of the chocolate, cut into small chunks, and stir into the mixture.

Grease a square baking tin (roughly 20cm) with a little oil and line with greaseproof paper. Pour the brownie mixture into the tin and spread out evenly. Bake for about 20 to 25 minutes until cooked on the outside but still gooey in the middle. Leave to cool for about 5 minutes then turn out into a wire cooling rack. These will keep in an airtight container for 3-4 days, although they're so deliciously moreish they might not last that long…

Thai green curry with peas and broad beans

It's a fairly recent addition to British cuisine but Thai green curry has fast become one of the nation's favourite meals, probably because it's warming and comforting but not too heavy. It's also relatively easy to make and pretty healthy to boot. If you want to make a lighter version you can use coconut milk from a carton (the kind you'd pour over cereal or have in tea or coffee) instead of the canned variety. It can be tricky to find vegan Thai green curry paste (most of them contain fish sauce or shrimps) but the Blue Dragon and Geo Organics versions are a good option.

30 minutes | Serves 4

Ingredients

– 200g fresh peas, shelled (or use frozen)
– 200g fresh broad beans, shelled (or use frozen)
– 300g spinach (or half a big bag)
– 1 small onion or 2 shallots, peeled and diced
– 2 medium carrots, diced
– 1 tbsp sesame or coconut oil (olive or vegetable are fine too)
– 1 tsp fresh ginger, finely chopped
– 2 garlic cloves, peeled and finely chopped
– Pinch of salt
– 2 tbsp Thai green curry paste
– 1 can (400ml) coconut milk
– 1 to 2 tsp maple syrup
– The juice of 1 lime
– 1 to 2 tsp soy sauce
– Handful of parsley or coriander, chopped
– 425g brown rice

Start by cooking the rice. Bring a large pot of water to the boil, add the rinsed rice and continue boiling for 30 minutes. Meanwhile, warm a large saucepan or wok over a medium heat and when it's hot, add the oil.

Cook the onion, ginger and garlic with a sprinkle of salt for about 5 minutes, stirring frequently. Add the carrots and cook for 3 minutes, stirring occasionally. Then add the curry paste and cook (keep stirring!) for 2 minutes.

Pour the coconut milk into the pan, along with half a mug of water and the maple syrup. Bring the mixture to a simmer then reduce the heat and after 5 minutes, add the peas and broad beans. Cook for another 5–6 minutes until the vegetables are tender and cooked through. Add a little water and stir through the spinach, and cook for another minute or so – or until it's wilted.

Remove the curry from the heat and season with the lime juice and soy sauce. Divide the rice and curry into bowls and garnish with herbs and sliced red chilies, if you like. If you have leftovers, this is great heated up the next day.

Potato gratin

Take one mouthful of this creamy classic and you'll immediately want another – and then another. This French dish, sometimes called potato dauphinoise, gets its name from gratiné, the word for crust or skin which forms over the potatoes when cooked. Although it requires a fair bit of slicing and takes a while to cook, this is definitely worth the wait. In days gone by, this was cooked on a Sunday before church and would be ready by the time families got home. The traditional recipe uses double cream but this version combines oat milk with flour and hot stock for a rich and velvety texture, although any plant milk works well.

1 hour 30 minutes | Serves 4

Ingredients

– 650g potatoes, sliced thinly
– 2 tbsp olive oil, plus extra for greasing
– 2 garlic cloves, peeled and finely diced
– 500ml oat milk
– 250ml vegetable stock
– 3 tbsp plain flour
– 3-4 tbsp nutritional yeast flakes
– 1 tsp salt
– 1 tsp white wine vinegar

First of all, make the sauce. Heat the oil in a large saucepan over a medium heat, then add the garlic and sauté for 2-3 minutes, until soft and translucent. Add the flour and salt and stir rapidly. Cook for a minute, then gradually add the plant milk and hot stock and stir through, then add the yeast flakes and vinegar. Cook for another 5 minutes, stirring all the while. Try to get out all the lumps if you can.

Now, turn the oven on to 200C. Slice the potatoes thinly, then in a colander rinse and spread onto a clean tea towel to dry – doing this removes the starch. Use a little oil to grease a casserole or large ovenproof dish. Spread a layer of potatoes along the bottom and cover with some of the sauce. Add another layer of potatoes and add more sauce then place a final layer of potatoes on top and season with salt and pepper. Cover with a lid or foil and place on the top shelf of the oven. Bake for 45 minutes then remove the lid or foil and bake for another 25–30 minutes, until golden brown. For a really crisp topping, place it under the grill (lid off) for the final 5 minutes.

Cawl

The national dish of Wales is hearty and healthy and the closest you can get to a cwtch in food form. Mum would make this once in a blue moon and when she did, it was such a comforting treat.

This almost stew-like soup is traditionally made with lamb but I've used braised tofu for a meaty taste and texture. To make a cawl of something means to mess something up, but don't worry: that's almost impossible with this recipe, although be patient because this will take a while to cook.

It's lovely served with some crusty bread and vegan cheese – and if you want the flavours to really develop, you can keep it in the fridge for a few days before reheating and serving. It also freezes really well – handy if you're making a big batch.

1 hour 30 minutes, plus extra time for preparing the tofu | Serves 4

Ingredients

For the tofu

- 1 x 400g block firm tofu
- 1 tbsp Marmite
- 1 tsp vegetable stock powder
- 100ml boiling water

For the cawl

- 50g pearl barley
- 1 medium onion, peeled and diced
- 3 bay leaves
- 2-3 large potatoes, quartered (or 2-3 baby new potatoes, halved)
- 1 large leek, finely sliced
- 2-3 sprigs of thyme
- 1 small swede, peeled and chopped into medium-sized chunks
- 2-3 carrots, peeled and chopped
- 2 tbsp olive oil
- 1 litre vegetable stock
- Salt and pepper

Take the tofu and use kitchen roll or a clean tea towel to blot and absorb all its water. Take two heavy wooden chopping boards and place on either side of the block to 'press' it and absorb excess moisture. If you can, put something heavy, like a hardback book, on top of the chopping board to weigh it down further. Leave for at least 30 minutes then slice into medium-sized chunks. Now, make your marinade by mixing together the Marmite, stock powder and water. Pour into a large dish, then coat both sides of the tofu strips with the mixture and leave to marinate for at least 30 minutes, or longer if you can.

Heat 1 tbsp oil in a pan over a medium heat and fry the onions for five minutes. Add all the other ingredients apart from the tofu and leeks and pour over the hot stock. Season with salt and pepper, then bring to the boil, reduce the heat and simmer for 20-25 minutes, stirring frequently.

While the soup is still simmering, heat 1 tbsp oil in a large frying pan over a medium heat. Fry the tofu for 10 minutes, until brown, turning every so often. Pour the leftover marinade into the pot with the cawl and when it's been cooking for 25 minutes, add the fried tofu and leeks and cook for another 15-20 minutes and add more stock if needed. When it's cooked, remove the bay leaves and thyme and serve with crusty bread.

Baked apples

This is something that Mum used to pop in the oven on a cold night and this quick and easy pudding is a lovely way to enjoy apples. The smell of allspice will always take me back to this dish. It's sublime and simple (like the best dishes often are) and it works all year round - just swap the sultanas for summer berries in the warmer months. It can also be enjoyed at breakfast time, perhaps with oats and some coconut yogurt.

30-35 minutes | Serves 2

Ingredients

– 2 cooking apples
– 70g sultanas
– 50g brown sugar
– 1 tsp ground allspice
– 1 tsp ground cinnamon
– 25g vegan margarine (optional)

Preheat the oven to 200C. Using an apple corer (don't use a knife as this can be very dangerous), remove the cores from both apples and place in a shallow ovenproof dish. In a bowl, mix the sugar, sultanas, allspice and cinnamon. Use your fingers to push the sultana mixture into each apple. Top with the margarine, if you like, then place on the middle shelf of the oven and bake for 20-25 minutes. Serve with vegan cream or vegan ice cream – or just as it is.

Sweet potato Kievs

As a treat or when Mum didn't have time to cook, she'd pick something up from Marks and Spencer – and we'd often have chicken Kiev, which was the first ever chilled ready meal. This was one of my favourite meals as a child, although to be honest, I had many. This veggie version uses sweet potato and lentils instead of chicken but still has a river of garlic butter that oozes out from the middle. You'll need a bit of patience to make this but I think you'll find that it's worth it.

2 hours | Serves 4

Ingredients

For the kievs

– 400g sweet potato, peeled and chopped into medium-sized pieces
– 200g green lentils
– 50g sesame seeds
– 50g sunflower seeds
– 70g Brazil nuts, very finely chopped
– 100g breadcrumbs
– 1 shallot or small onion, peeled and finely diced
– 4 sprigs of thyme
– 1 tbsp balsamic vinegar
– 1 tbsp olive oil
– Salt and pepper

For the garlic butter

– 150g vegan margarine, at room temperature
– 4 garlic cloves, peeled and finely chopped
– 4 tsp garlic, finely chopped

For the coating

– 4 tbsp plain flour
– 8 tbsp water
– 2 tbsp olive oil
– Salt and pepper
– 200g breadcrumbs

First of all, make your garlic butter. Cream together the margarine, garlic and parsley, place in a container and put in the fridge (or freezer) while you're making everything else

Bring a large pan of water to the boil and add the sweet potato and lentils. Boil for 15-20 minutes until tender. Drain well, mash and leave to cool. Use a food processor to blend the nuts (or chop very finely) and the seeds, although they can be left whole. Use a food processor or grater to make breadcrumbs. Mix all the ingredients, together with the thyme, shallot, balsamic vinegar and oil and season with salt and pepper.

Divide the potato mixture into four and shape into large patty shapes. Take the garlic butter from the fridge and divide into four. Make a dint in the centre of each kiev and pop in a portion of butter. Form the potato mixture around the garlic butter and cover so that you end up with a flattened cake shape. Place on a plate in the fridge for 30-45 minutes.

Preheat the oven to 200C (gas mark 6). Make your coating by mixing the flour, water and oil in a bowl. Using a pastry brush (or spoon), coat one side of the kiev with the flour mixture then evenly spread over the breadcrumbs. Do the same on the other side and around the edges for all four kievs. Using a spatula, carefully place the kievs onto a baking tray and place on the top shelf of the oven. Cook for 25-30 minutes, turning halfway through, then serve.

Pistachio ice cream

Italian café culture thrived in the Welsh Valleys during the twentieth century and it's still a big part of the community. Growing up, I made frequent trips to visit my grandmother in Aberdare, and with my pocket money I devoured Servini's ice cream sundaes before going to Woolworths to buy some pick and mix, or if I was feeling particulary grown-up, a Forever Friends diary.

My sister Jess loved pistachio ice cream (she still does), a flavour that can be hard to track down these days. I have fond memories of that subtly sweet, nutty gelato so I decided to make my own. This dairy-free version is easy peasy to make, and it's no-churn, too.

40 minutes, plus freezing and thawing | Serves 4

Ingredients

– 150g pistachios, shelled (plus extra for decorating)
– 2 x 400ml cans coconut milk
– 200ml plant milk
– 2 tbsp plain flour
– 50ml maple syrup
– 2 tsp almond extract
– 2 tsp natural green food colouring

Put all the ingredients (except the food colouring) into a food processor. Blend on high until smooth then pour the mixture into a large bowl and stir through the food colouring.

Pour into a plastic container and top with some chopped pistachios. Freeze for 12 hours or overnight. When you're ready to serve the ice cream, remove from the freezer and allow to thaw for 15-20 minutes (or longer if the ice cream has been frozen for a few days. Mash with a potato masher for a softer consistency, then top with the chopped pistachios and enjoy.

Meatless moussaka

A Greek classic and one of my go to comfort foods because Mum made this a lot when we were growing up. It goes down just as well on a balmy summer's evening (so rare in this country) or on a wet and windy night. With a rich lentil base and creamy béchamel sauce, you'd never guess that it's vegan.

1 hour, 15 minutes | Serves 4

Ingredients

For the lentil base

200g green lentils, rinsed and drained
1 large aubergine, sliced into thin rounds
1 green pepper, thinly sliced
1 red pepper, thinly sliced
2 x 400g cans tomatoes, chopped or plum
1 large onion, peeled and diced
2 garlic cloves, peeled and chopped finely
4-5 tsp tomato purée
3 tbsp olive oil
1 cinnamon stick (or 1 tsp of cinnamon powder)
4 tsp parsley, chopped finely
2-3 tsp mint, chopped finely (or 2 tsp dried)

For the béchamel sauce

500ml soya, nut or oat milk
2 bay leaves
1 onion, peeled and roughly sliced
4 tbsp plain flour
3 tbsp olive oil
1½ tsp vegetable stock powder
¼ tsp nutmeg, grated
Salt and black pepper

In a large pan, heat 1 tbsp oil over a low to medium heat, then add the onions and garlic and fry for five minutes. Now add the lentils, peppers, tomatoes, tomato purée, parsley and cinnamon, plus 300ml water. Season generously with salt and pepper. Reduce the heat, cover the pan with a lid and simmer for 30 minutes, stirring occasionally.

While the lentil sauce is cooking, make your béchamel sauce. Place all the ingredients, except for the oil and flour into a saucepan and mix together. Bring to the boil, then remove from the heat and set aside and allow to cool. Remove the onion and bay leaves using a slotted spoon. In a separate saucepan, mix together the flour and oil with a dash of milk until you have a smooth paste. Gradually, pour in the milk mixture, whisking or stirring constantly. Place the pan on a high heat and bring to the boil, whisking or stirring all the time, until the mixture thickens to a smooth sauce. Make it as thick as you like by adding extra flour – or if you want a thinner sauce, add more milk. Season with salt and pepper and remove from the heat. Remove the cinnamon stick and discard.

Preheat the oven to 200C. In a large bowl, mix the aubergine slices with 2 tbsp of oil, making sure to coat each slice. Season with salt and pepper. Heat a large pan over a medium heat and fry the aubergine on both sides for 2-3 minutes, or until golden brown.

Take an ovenproof dish and layer the lentil sauce at the base, then layer over the aubergine slices and the chopped mint. Now pour over the béchamel sauce and spread evenly.

Place on the top shelf of the oven and bake for 20-25 minutes.

Conversion charts

Dry weights

Metric	Imperial	Metric	Imperial
5g	¼oz	400g	¼oz
8/10g	⅓oz	425g	⅓oz
15g	½oz	450g	½oz
20g	¾oz	475g	¾oz
25g	1oz	500g	1oz
30/35g	1¼oz	550g	1¼oz
40g	1½oz	600g	1½oz
50g	2oz	625g	2oz
60/70g	2½oz	650g	2½oz
75/85/90g	3oz	675g	3oz
100g	3½oz	700g	3½oz
110/120g	4oz	750g	4oz
125/130g	4½oz	800g	4½oz
135/140/150g	5oz	850g	5oz
170/175g	6oz	900g	6oz
200g	7oz	950g	7oz
225g	8oz	1kg	8oz
250g	9oz	1.1kg	9oz
265g	9½oz	1.25kg	9½oz
275g	10oz	1.3/1.4kg	10oz
300g	11oz	1.5kg	11oz
325g	11½oz	1.75/1.8kg	11½oz
350g	12oz	2kg	12oz
375g	13oz		

Liquids

Metric	Imperial	Cups
15ml	½fl oz	1 tbsp
20ml	¾fl oz	
30ml	1fl oz	⅛ cup
60ml	2fl oz	¼ cup
75ml	2½fl oz	
90ml	3fl oz	⅓ cup
100ml	3½fl oz	
120ml	4fl oz	½ cup
135ml	4½fl oz	
160ml	5fl oz	⅔ cup
180ml	6fl oz	¾ cup
210ml	7fl oz	
240ml	8fl oz	1 cup
265ml	9fl oz	
300ml	10fl oz	1¼ cups
350ml	12fl oz	1½ cups
415ml	14fl oz	
480ml	16fl oz / 1 pint	2 cups
530ml	18fl oz	2¼ cups
1 litre	32fl oz	4 cups

Diolch!

It's a dream come true to share my love of food with you in *The Occasional Vegan*. Writing a book doesn't happen on its own and I'm very lucky to know some wonderful people who have really been there for me in the past year.

Thank you to the team at Seren, and especially to Mick for taking a chance on me.

Thank you to Laetitia who helped me so much in the early planning of *The Occasional Vegan* and to my dear friend Becky for all her enthusiasm and encouragement.

This book wouldn't look so beautiful if it weren't for Manon and her eye for a good photograph. You're so talented and I can't wait to see what you work on next.

Thank you to everyone who went out of their way to test my recipes. I'm name checking you all because each and every one of you helped make this a better book. So, bon appetit to Maria, Mikey, Rosie, Jane, Sareta, Lleucu, Elin, Amy and Matt, Amo, Kacie, Sarah and Nick, Claire, Aled and baby Joe, Michelle and Jeremy, Rachel, Simon, Mandy, Becky and Philippa, Lois and Luke, Louise, Rose, Gemma, Lynsey and Gwilym, Jude, Sarah (another one!), Nicky, Alison, Edwina, and Rhian and Duncan. Diolch yn fawr.

Thank you to my amazing friends, old and new, for all your love and support over the years – and for patiently standing by as I photographed every single meal.

Kieron and Seren: you fill my life with so much light and laughter and I love you both very much. Thank you for putting up with me.

Finally, a huge thank you to my family: Jess, Lucy, Fred, Vianne and Paul – and of course, Mum. You've always fed me with food and love and I'll never forget that.

Index